River Crossings®

Weekly blogs from a missionary in Thailand

Marsha Woods

River Crossings
Copyright © 2011 by Marsha G Woods

International Trade Paper Edition

This title is also available at www.amazon.com
Requests for information should be directed to info@martonpublishing.com

ISBN: 978-0-9834091-1-3

All rights reserved. No part of this publication may be reproduced, stored in a retrieval system, or transmitted in any form or by any means - electronic, mechanical, photocopy, recording or any other - except for brief quotations in printed reviews, without the prior permission of the author.

Scriptures taken from the Holy Bible,
New International Version®, NIV®.
Copyright © 1973, 1978, 1984 by Biblica, Inc.™
Used by permission of Zondervan.
All rights reserved worldwide. www.zondervan.com

You cannot cross a river twice.

The river will be different.

You will be different.

- Heraclitus of Ephesus, Greek philosopher,
c.535 BC - 475 BC

Foreword

Marsha and Tony Woods had been missionaries for 35 years, serving in three African countries, in Japan, Hong Kong and Australia, when they were asked to go to Thailand. For them, this was something altogether different, and thanks to the kind of technology they were only just beginning to grow into, Marsha decided to make a blog about it. A web site was created, and each week Marsha would write a paragraph or two about life in Bangkok. The response was so great, she began to see this as a ministry, sharing insights with people all over the world, who in turn would share a few of their own. The word spread rapidly, and soon people started asking for different formats to make the blog easier to access. A mailing list was built for those who had mastered the mystery of email but had yet to make the stretch to the World Wide Web. There was even a contingent of folks who had no interest in computers at all, but thanks to kids, grandkids and friends were given a weekly hard copy of the blog which was then passed around to missionary support groups from Texas to Queensland, Australia.

The blog continued from the middle of 2009 until the end of 2010, when the Woods were asked to move yet again, this time back to Japan, where they had already spent 20 years, raising three children and burying one. The story didn't end there; they had barely unpacked their suitcases when they found themselves caught up in Japan's worst earthquake on record, followed by the most destructive tsunami ever. The area hit hardest was the northern town of Sendai, where their son Trevor's grave is located. At the time of this writing, Marsha continues to chronicle their experiences at www.mywoods.net as they work together with the Japanese people to try and bring hope to over half a million people who have quite literally lost everything. This book, though, will focus on those 18 months in Bangkok. Each blog will include a Scripture reference which hopefully will direct the reader to a devotional theme for the day.

I pray that these pages will bring a blessing to you as they have to many others, and especially to me. I have to admit to a certain advantage, having shared Marsha's life for these past 42 years. I've seen her in the better, and in the worse, and til death do us part I can testify that she is one of the most spiritually honest people I have ever known. As you read her words, you will see as I have that here is a child of God who faces each day as a child should, looking up the Father for comfort, for encouragement and for a job to do which will honor Him and His Kingdom. This book is the product of one such calling. May it inspire you as it has me.

Tony Woods

1. From Mars Hill
(July 6th)

Yesterday Tony and I watched the sun set over Athens from atop Mars Hill, at the base of the Acropolis. Back in the first century, the area was known as Areopagus, and it's such a rocky place that the inhabitants had literally carved out walkways, steps, and the foundations of their houses in the granite. One industrious resident even built his entire home back in the rock, complete with door, window, and carvings on the walls! Standing on the spot where most agree would have been the Apostle Paul's speaking platform, I recalled his words, recorded in Acts 17: "Men of Athens! I see that in every way you are very religious. For as I walked around and looked carefully at your objects of worship, I even found an altar with this inscription: TO AN UNKNOWN GOD. Now what you worship as something unknown I am going to proclaim to you."

And so he did. Many heard him that day, and a few believed, including a man by the name of Dionysus, a member of the local Council, and a woman named Damaris. Other writings outside the Bible tell us that they went on to build the first church in Athens.

What has always intrigued me about Paul's proclamation, though, was the observation that the people to whom he spoke were "very religious". I think the same can be said of a lot of folks today. Tonight we're getting on a plane for the last leg of our journey back to Bangkok, and boy, would the peopled there have "amened" Paul that day on Mars Hill! The Thai are some of the most religious people I've ever known, with temples erected by law within every building constructed (The Baptist church has received an exception to the law, since we have a God already). These people talk freely and sincerely about the world of the spirits, and man's obligation to them. The problem is, most of them have never met the UNKNOWN GOD Paul talked about. And that's what draws us back to Thailand.

But as I think about it, there're a lot of similarities between Thais, Athenians, and you and me. We've all been blessed with an innate desire to know God (see also the presence of "religion" everywhere you go in the world), but somehow we've forgotten Who He is. I'd like to hear from you: what's going around as "religion" where you live, and how does it compare with the One Who placed the longing in our hearts to start with? And what can you do about it?

For as I walked around and looked carefully at your objects of worship, I even found an altar with this inscription: TO AN UNKNOWN GOD. Now what you worship as something unknown I am going to proclaim to you. (Acts 17:23)

2. Last Leg to Bangkok!
(July 13th)

I heard an interesting story last week in Athens. Some of you may know it, so don't give away the ending!

It seems in 490 B.C. the Persians came to defeat the Greeks yet again in a small town south of Athens. However, this time, by some miraculous turn of events, the Greeks won handily, actually routing the Persians forever. A guy named Pheidyppides was so excited he RAN to tell the good news to the people waiting in Athens. When he arrived, he shouted "Nenikekamen!" and proceeded to drop dead of exhaustion. You see, he had run 26 miles without a break from the battle ground town of... you guessed it, "Marathon". "Nenikekamen" has since been shortened to "Nike" and the meaning is "Victory". The rest of the story is history.

After so many months of being in limbo, we have finally laced up our shoes and begun the "marathon" of our great race to announce "Victory" to the people of Thailand. We arrived Monday night in Bangkok after about 20 hours of travelling and transferred directly to Chiang Mai in the north where we've had a exciting week of meetings with our mission and all our new co-workers.

Now, as you're reading this, we'll be flying back to Bangkok to find our home which we've never seen, unpack the boxes that we've mailed from here and there and start language school next week. We feel that we're already tired and we haven't even passed the first mile marker. We've had a couple of bits of bad news over the last week, which make us want to turn away from the goal so that we can sit down and worry, and on top of that, we can't seem to put a sentence together in English, much less Thai… but we have to remember the "Nike" message and the exciting race ahead. Thanks for praying for us, thanks for being in the race with us.

Paul, in the Bible, knew of Pheidyppides. In fact, it was an old story when he heard it 600 years after it happened. Maybe that's why he wrote, "and let us run with perseverance the race marked out for us, and let us fix our eyes on Jesus, the author and perfecter of our faith. (Hebrews 12, 1 and 2)

May your running be enjoyable this week and we'll see you next week at the water station!

Marsha and Tony

Do you not know that in a race all the runners run, but only one gets the prize? Run in such a way as to get the prize. (1 Corinthians 9:24)

3. First Week in Bangkok
(July 19th)

Well, as I write this blog, I'm sitting at a desk, with my OLD computer hooked up, almost feeling like I'm at home.

The week started off with us being dropped unceremoniously at our new digs, way way out in a neighborhood we'd never been to when we lived here before. It's much more of a suburb than when we stayed here for a short time last year, and so we don't have the same way of relating to our environment. Yes, there's a big store like a 'Walmart' just a few blocks away, but where is my satay man or the fruit lady? How will I get clean clothes with no maid? (don't laugh). It's amazing how you can feel so lost when you never really 'had' it before.

The mission had graciously put some random furniture in for us to use and as we started working I almost cried when Tony unpacked a box and found our missing Oswald Chambers devotional book. We had accused family and friends of mislaying it for us, when as usual, it was our own over-packing that had 'lost' it. Tony said, "Well, since we finally found it, let's see what he says for today".

July 13th:

"Over and over God has to remove our friends in order to bring Himself in their place, and that is where we faint and fall and get discouraged… Before I can say "I saw also the Lord," there must be something corresponding to God in my character. It must be God first, God second, and God third until the life is faced steadily with God and no one else is of any account whatever… Keep paying the price, Let God see that you are willing to live up to the vision".

I don't know about you, but that hit me right between the 'starting to want a nice wobbly cry' eyes! So we 'pulled our socks up', got busy de-mystifying the life at THIS END of Bangkok, (we could tell you stories!) and started our pre-school sound pattern lessons. Now we can say we've eyeballed all 44 consonants and 24 vowels, and Tony's happy to find that a few can't be pronounced without SMILING. The teacher assures him that he can smile, but he has to lose the Texas drawl. The teacher also says I need more confidence, because I end every sound with a rising "question" tone and that, of course, changes the meaning of the sound completely. Heaven help us!

We will start formal study this Wednesday. Who can say how we'll do. Only God knows, but then we have to remind ourselves, "only God matters".

Keep the faith, and hopefully we'll check in next week!

Jesus replied, "No one who puts his hand to the plow and looks back is fit for service in the kingdom of God."
(Luke 9:62)

4. Tears in the Paint Can
(July 26th)

This last week we got an interesting phone call from our son Nathan and his lovely wife, Kylie.
It wasn't till the next afternoon when I was painting some drawers to match our other bedroom cabinets that it hit me. I was getting a bit bored with just the 'whop whop' of the fan and the smell of the paint fumes so I decided to pop in a CD that we'd found in a pile of stuff left by the last folks in this apartment.
Suddenly it was 1981 and I'd just flown in from Japan to the states to adopt a perfect little two day old boy. While I was there, I had randomly bought a cassette tape of some new band who didn't know how to spell their name, and I loved it so much I played it almost non stop for a year.
Now as I began to listen to the all too familiar strains of Abba (with the backwards B) all those feelings from way back then began to come together. I saw a tear land in the paint and had to sit down and collect myself. Where did my little boy go? How could anyone have brought his dad and I so much joy and now... Who was this MAN calling to tell me that HE's going to become a father? How could my little boy be a father when he was just reaching up to me out of the crib a few years ago? Do

Kylie's folks have the same dejavu' feelings about their little girl growing up?

Where did the time go? When did he grow up? How could he possibly love anything as much as we love him? How does this 'grandparent' thing work anyway? How magnificent is our God that He gives the ones we love the most... something to love even more?

Ahhhh.......... We're going to be GRANDPARENTS. My mind is still blown... which, of course isn't a good thing since we're swinging into full time language school!

But on that note, we're happy to report that there have been no disasters yet. We're actually doing rather well, but after only two formal days, it may be a bit soon to call it! Tony and I are in separate classes, each having about four or five different nationalities, English not being a common language. Once everybody figures out what the teacher is saying, I'm sure they'll take off. Anyway, as my grandmother, who I'm beginning to understand loved me dearly, used to say about most anything that was productive, "It sure beats hanging around the drug store!"

Have a great week as you celebrate with us!
Marsha and Tony, the Ancient Ones.

Children's children are a crown to the aged, and parents are the pride of their children. (Proverbs 17:6)

5. Anniversary Time!
(August 2nd)

This weekend was our 40th anniversary. Who would have guessed God would bless us with such a wonderful marriage, two best friends, for all these years.

To celebrate, we decided to stay at a hotel nearby. To get there, you have to cross a rather grotty slum from us, but when/if you get through, you break out into a different world of luxury and opulence. Bangkok's like that. I couldn't manage to attach the picture we took, but there's a bronze plaque on the cornerstone of the hotel we stayed at that read: "In honor of Mr. Chuvit Davis Kamolvisit, and dedicated to the Lord Jesus Christ."

Isn't that amazing? Isn't it heartening to see such a statement a block from a rather hopeless slum?

Well, we did some research. If you'll google Mr. Chuvit Davis Kamolvisit, you'll find that he's a major slum landlord and has made his billions mostly on the massage parlor (the nefarious kind) industry. "Oh," you think hopefully, he's made the Lord Jesus Christ the lord of his life and has thought to mention it here on the side of his hotel. Think again. Last year he was up on battery charges for belting a journalist who insulted his masculinity.

Do we sometimes think that 'keeping the bases covered'

is enough? What did Jesus say in the New Testament, "Not everyone who says 'Lord, Lord' will enter the kingdom of heaven."

Looking back over the past 40 years, I'd like to think that our lives have been REALLY dedicated to the LORD Jesus Christ. (I learned the word for "really" this week, and it's "jing jing, so we've been having fun saying that.) Pray for us as we try to lay on the steam this week in preparation for Nathan and Kylie's visit on the 9th of August! We've got to keep up with our studies, even though we'll be in HEAVEN having them here!

…and maybe say a prayer for Mr. Chavut; that he'll find the one and only Lord of his life.

"Not everyone who says to me, 'Lord, Lord,' will enter the kingdom of heaven, but only he who does the will of my Father who is in heaven. (Matthew 7:21)

6. Body Parts
(August 9th)

Have you ever stood on the beach and let the waves lap at your feet? You might notice that after a few waves you feet have disappeared and even though they're still there, they're now buried in sand. Well, that's like riding the commuter train every morning in Bangkok. You get in, which in itself looks like an undoable task till others start pushing from behind. Then with each consecutive station, the 'waves' of people push you further and further into the sands of humanity. By now your feet have disappeared as well as your husband and you pray for something to lean against or at least a place to hang on. That's where I found myself the other day. I was blissfully shoved up against one of the poles in the middle of the car. This is considered to be a lucky break, because now you have a foundation to brace yourself when the sways and turns come. Of course there are always bumps on the pole of one sort or another, joints, patches, etc. The top half of my anatomy had become 'one with the pole', and it was all good. After a few stops, I casually noticed the rather red and uncomfortable face of a student standing directly opposite me at the pole. It was then that I realized that one of the 'bumps' was actually his hand, firmly buried in my small but amply imposing chest.

Of course, the good missionary that I am, I jumped back enough to release the pressure so that he could disengage his hand. Then I said in my very best Thai, an emphatic "Khap-khoon—MAAK Kha!... He got off at the next stop, right before I realized that instead of saying "Sorry, excuse me!" I'd said... "Thank you SO MUCH!" I'll ride in a different car from now on.

Hope you have a great week. When you read this I'll have a daughter who has left her teenage years behind and my son and daughter in love (and baby makes three) who will be with us for ten days tearing up Thailand while we continue to try to figure out how to say "sorry" instead of "thank you!".

God Bless,

Marsha and Tony

"Brothers and fathers, listen now to my defense." When they heard him speak to them in Aramaic, they became very quiet. (Acts 22:1-2)

7. Getting More Than Ice Cream
(August 16th)

Let me tell you about a girl I met this week.
Her name is Fon (pronounced 'fawn') and she came to see me with another girl I was meeting for the first time. Let me back up. The "other girl" had rung me the night before. She got my name from a mutual acquaintance of ours in Japan. She is new in town and a bit lonely, so I said, "Look, even though my kids are coming for a visit this week and between them and language study we don't have a minute to spare, come to the Dairy Queen on Sunday afternoon after your church service and we'll at least get to see your face."
A few of our folks like to go there after the three hour Thai church service for a taste of "home". She did, and brought her new friend that she had met on the bus going to church. Fon sat down and seemed relieved that a few of us around the table could speak a few words of Thai. She began to share her story with a colleague who thankfully has more Thai skills than I have (he's been here something like 20 years). "I want to explore Christianity but I'm afraid," she began. "I went to several temples (Buddhist) but I felt nothing, only a coldness." "Because I work nights," she went on, "I usually can't sleep on my nights off, but I asked God that if He wanted

me to know Him, He'd have to help me sleep. That night, I slept like a baby and got up and went to Church. When I walked in the door I felt a strange warmth, even before I'd met anyone. Now is my third week to go and I'm feeling more and more like there's a God who loves me!" I shouted out, half joking, "Give that girl a Bible!".

Without a glance, the colleague reached in his wife's bag, pulled out HER Thai/English Bible and handed it to the girl. She was stunned. Tony grabbed it back away from her and quickly underlined some of HIS favorite verses and then gave it back. As we left, I thought to myself, "This is what missions is all about: being at the right place at the right time and being sensitive to the leading of the Holy Spirit, Who sometimes breaks through what may seem to us as "common sense".

This colleague, (who incidentally is our business manager and a bit of a penny pincher) makes me proud to be 'one of the team'. We're with our kids from Australia this week, and having a ball! Pray for Fon and also that we'll 'graduate' from the first module at language school this week! Happy trails, do something outside of yourself, it's fun!

Marsha and Tony

But when they arrest you, do not worry about what to say or how to say it. At that time you will be given what to say… (Matthew 10:19)

8. As seen in this week's blog
(August 23rd)

In Bangkok we don't have a car. That means we have a variety of transportation options at our disposal. We try to walk most everywhere, but of course we often go further than the neighborhood. Most of the time I feel quite blessed to be able to raise my hand wherever I am and a sleek A/C taxi pulls up. Then the fun begins: will he speak any English, will he understand my Thai, will he go 160km/90miles an hour thru the streets, or will he go the 'back way' thus running up the fare? Other modes for movement are the famous 'sky train' that is clean and cool, but bastioned above hundreds of steps and it's not all that expansive, so it limits where you'll be going. There are buses and a subway but we haven't really demystified those yet. Another option is a boat, and that's what we needed last night.

Apparently our little street floods every time there's a sprinkle of rain. As I walked out last night to go to a meeting, I picked up several items of rubbish that had floated into our yard the other day. Then as the prayer meeting droned on, the rain poured, and as we approached our 'soy' or street in the taxi, we knew we'd be doing what we've come to think of as normal: WADING. Last night it was only over our knees, but it has been thigh deep before. I never thought standing before the mirror for that last minute check before leaving would involve, "can I swim in this?"

I guess this problem won't go away so we'll just buy some more Dettol/Lysol. Ain't life grand?

On this 'transportation topic' I want to direct your attention to the picture on the blog, click on "the world of the woods". There you can see Tony "driving" an elephant.

You can also see how I feel most days by the look on my face. It says, "What in the world are we doing? HOW are we going to get this pachyderm off the tree?"

That pretty well sums up our mood these days. We have a few skills now in the Thai language, but where we're going with it is still a mystery. Our work and our future is still undefined as we struggle with the language. We experience small victories every day (not unlike finally getting ON the elephant)... but now we wonder...

Pray with us as the plan unfolds. We feel that God wants us here; we're just having to remember that it's a day by day walk, and God only knows what the Grand Plan is! Meanwhile we enjoy life, LOVED the visit from our kids and are forging on!

May your elephant be cooperative this week!

We live by faith, not by sight. (2 Corinthians 5:7)

9. Big Steps
(August 30th)

Well, it's been a week! We were "promoted" to Thai language level two and on Monday new classes began with the same breakneck speed that they seem to enjoy. We have new teachers, new rooms and a few new classmates who seem to be barely out of diapers. At least it's clear that their brain cells are at least half the age of mine. I, on the other hand, vacillate between being on top of the game and dragging along behind with no idea what's happening. Neither of us have actually cried yet (Tony DID decide to quit one hour but then had tremendous success the next). It's definitely a 'day by day' experience.

Some of you expressed concerns last week about our blog, saying we should come home and just quit trying so hard. Part of us says, "Yeah; why are we killing ourselves, when we could probably take early retirement and start living the dream back Down Under with the soon-to-arrive grandkid?" But then we think, "wait a minute; life is ALWAYS a challenge, one way or the other." At least in this situation we get to choose our method of torture! Oh, but there's more! Last week Tony and I did a bad thing and popped into a little Japanese worship service which meets in a hotel around the corner. We're supposed to be attending Thai church to further our language, but hey, everybody needs a break, eh? It was so wonderful, and maybe really a 'God Thing' as well. It so happens, their pastor is old and sick and back in Japan for quite a while. They were just wondering what they would do, and were praying about it when we stepped in the door. There were a few awkward moments as they thought we had come to the wrong place, but then when Tony stood and introduced us in Japanese, mentioning that we had served in Japan for 20 years, and pastored a small church there, we saw the personification of that great Aussie word: "Gobsmackered."

Well, talk about an instant feeling of being loved (OK OK, I know it's the 'warm body' syndrome, but anyway) by Tuesday they had had a meeting and called Tony as pastor! ha. So sweet, really. Anyway, we've explained that our number one "job" at present is the Thai language, but today when we visited again (shhhh) I saw Tony taking mental notes of guitar pickup amps and members' names, etc. etc. Who knows what God is providing for us to do! Don't misunderstand: we still have our eyes on that back porch and rocking chair, but wouldn't it be great if we could see a real live Japanese church come about before we pack it in?

We've also settled on our fashion attire for the flooded street. (See last week's blog post if you don't know what

I'm talking about) I really didn't get freaked till Tony used the word "Sewer"... anyway, we decided on two heavy duty garbage bags each (Tony will be responsible for carrying these at all times since HE said the word "sewer!") We deliberated about ONE bag each and just doing the gunny sack hop all the way home but at our age and with the unevenness of the street, we'd probably end up nose diving into the... sewer. All is well, and we're ready for the next deluge. We've been lucky this week, only one 'episode'.

We hear good things from you about your lives and challenges. Keep up the good work and we'll try to do the same.

Tony and Marsha

Whether you turn to the right or to the left, your ears will hear a voice behind you, saying, "This is the way; walk in it." (Isaiah 30:21)

10. Say What??
(September 6th)

We're coming into that dangerous stage of language study: the time when you know just enough to be understood, but not necessarily what you think you're communicating. Like for instance the other day when Tony told the motorcycle taxi driver he wanted to leave dog doo on his bike (Ghii with an upward inflection rather than Ghii with no inflection). The guy must have understood, since he gave Tony a ride home, but now we know why he was grinning so much!

Actually my literary creations are quite proper, if not exactly useful, like telling the teacher yesterday that I wanted her to take my refrigerator outside, please. Hey, you never know when a phrase like that might come in handy.

And come to think of it, I'm not the only one lacking all the information necessary for the situation. I remember a few years ago during the Sydney Olympics, we had some friends come out from the States to help with the Christian volunteers who were coordinating with the churches for evangelistic outreach. Now this couple specializes in 'jobs bordering on the impossible' so they were very much in demand. One night they were called to a church down south because their bus had broken down and John and Trudy needed to drop everything and run to fix it, as it was needed the next day. When they arrived, they found the church unlocked but apparently all the members had gone off to help at an Olympic event. The only one there was a rather scruffy gentleman sitting just inside the door out of the cold. They assumed he was the janitor or something, and said hello. Soon he asked them for a lift home, mentioning that it really wasn't very far but it'd be a big help if he didn't have to walk. They reasoned that they could at least do that for this old soldier of Christ, and since they had some time to kill, they agreed. After a few moments he indicated that if it wouldn't be too much trouble, could they help him load a refrigerator into the car as well... They did, albeit a bit puzzled, but figured that they just didn't understand Australian ways... and delivered him to his humble shack a few miles away.

The next morning the pastor apologized for not being there when they arrived, mentioning what a crazy evening it had been and commented casually that someone had actually stolen their refrigerator as well!... Language and culture, what a hoot! At least if someone here asks me to carry off the refrigerator, I'll know what they're saying!

Not much other riveting news. We're now halfway through module two of language study, with two weeks to go. In the meantime, opportunities for Japanese ministry have stopped knocking on the door and have begun drilling through the wall!... but more about that next week! Best of all, no floods the past ten days, so we're dry and happy!

PS They did get the fridge back. It pays when you know where the thief lives!

The disciples did not understand any of this. Its meaning was hidden from them, and they did not know what he was talking about. (Luke 18:34)

11. A Pat On The Head
(September 13th)

This weekend marks our seventh week of Thai study, and as we keep getting exposed to all the language we don't know yet, I figure in another month we should be totally illiterate! So, to celebrate the occasion and find some encouragement, Tony was blessed with the chance today to preach in Japanese. It's a small group (about 30) of Japanese and Thai people who meet at a hotel not five minutes walk from our house. (See "Big Steps" blog, August 30). I suppose a visit from royalty might have gotten a bigger response, but I don't think so. Having been without a "real live" pastor for so long, they were determined to make the most of the situation, asking for not only a sermon, but also Lord's Supper and a Benediction (reserved for the ordained in most Japanese churches). Tony gave it his best shot, pulled out the stops, and was like a kid in a candy store. Afterwards, a Thai lady came up to say that her Japanese husband was translating until about halfway through, when he started crying so much he couldn't go on! "I'm going home now to get the rest of the message after he settles down," she told Tony.

But here's the best part: unbeknownst to Tony, the sermon was recorded and this week will be on You Tube!

More on that when we hear (unless of course it's terrible, in which case you won't be hearing anything from us).

I know we're supposed to be full time into Thai language study, and we are – really. But once in awhile God seems to know what our childish hearts need, and today it was a pat on the head and a "good on ya!" So let me take this opportunity to say the same to all you out there who are struggling today with whatever it is the Lord has placed before you. I know Jesus promised us a yoke that was "easy", but the terrain we're plowing is not always so gentle. Disappointments, heartaches and the seemingly impossible challenges can make life look pretty grim. I don't need to tell most of you about the "prayer points" we've been sharing on a personal level. But let me just say that those shared burdens DO make us stronger, and somewhere down the line will give us reason to rejoice. For us, today was one of those moments. I pray that each of you will get a "good on ya" from someone you love real soon. Until then, here's one from me.

"Come to me, all you who are weary and burdened, and I will give you rest. Take my yoke upon you and learn from me, for I am gentle and humble in heart, and you will find rest for your souls. For my yoke is easy and my burden is light." (Matthew 11:28-30)

12. Speaking of Kangaroos...
(September 20th)

The word for 'acquaintance' in Thai is "Rook Jack". It's not spelled that way, but that's how it sounds. Funny sounding, really, so much so that I remember it by going back to that silly movie "Kangaroo Jack" and associating it with an 'acquaintance": just sorta 'hopping' in and out of your life.

We're on a break from language school (more about that below) so I've managed to tease open a very old and broken laptop of ours and get to the address file. I'm copying off the addresses, and some of our 'acquaintances' may be getting an email this week that says "Hey, do you remember us?" Truth is, I don't remember about a quarter of the people on the list. Who are they? Who WERE they to me? Tony sometimes muses that he wishes he'd stayed in the small Texas town he grew up in because then he'd really know everyone and wouldn't have to continually meet and lose friends.

Yesterday we went to a Japanese concert organized by the two groups we work with in town. We caught up with a lady and her family that were in the Japanese church in Hong Kong where we pastored briefly in 1996. We hadn't seen her in 14 years, but of course in the family of

Christ, it was just like yesterday. Then last night we had dinner with a missionary and reminisced about people we'd known and worked with years and years ago but are now lost to us. We were 'rook jacks' and now they've 'hopped' out of our lives... maybe till we meet again in heaven!

Do you think Jesus ever had 'rook jacks'? Is He the kind who would just get to know you and then leave the scene? You know the answer to that. Isn't it great that He never NOT knows you or worse yet, would ever FORGET you? The human in me wonders if He ever WISHES He didn't know some people... but of course you know that answer to that too!

I digress. On the news front, we've completed level two, but have decided (in mutual agreement with our teachers) that it would be a good thing if we take a break from the organized classroom and just spend this month 'getting it up to speed'. They say we've got the vocabulary and know the forms; we're just a bit slow off the block when we speak. So the plan starting tomorrow is to meet separately with a private tutor every day and PRACTICE PRACTICE PRACTICE for the next month. Without fellow classmates to keep us honest, I'm a little afraid that we'll get lazy, but on the other hand going nose to nose with a tutor may actually double our output! Pray for us. Tony's filling up his schedule with Japanese preaching and church work, which is exciting in itself, but we must consider it a distraction till we GET this LANGUAGE! As I said, we'd appreciate your prayers to stay on course.

Have a great week, fellow rook jacks. And wherever things take us, may we never lose track of the mob.

Tony and Marsha

Keep your lives free from the love of money and be content with what you have, because God has said, "Never will I leave you; never will I forsake you." (Hebrews 13:5)

13. Tailor Made
(September 27th)

You've heard the phrase 'what goes around comes around'. Today I'd like to tell you a story. It involves (1) two fresh faced young missionaries a lifetime ago and (2) Tony getting a suit made this week.

In the early 70's we were going out on our first assignment to Africa. We were young, we were enthusiastic and idealistic, we had NO IDEA! (but that's another story). There was a guy at the mission board to train us; he was quiet and unobtrusive. He rarely spoke up and although I remember him, I remember very little. I think he was old... maybe 40 or something. He didn't really make any huge impression on us except that he'd been somewhere in the world for a long time and maybe he didn't have the best clothes or the latest haircut. That's all.

Now fast forward to this last week. We were taking a short cut from our mission office to the train and were passing thru the red light district, as you do most anywhere in Bangkok. This time, however, what leapt out at me was a little tailor shop with the words emblazoned over the door, "Jesus Loves You!" and numerous fish stickers. Our friends stopped and chatted to an Indian man standing out in front and we moved on, us with our mouths hanging open.

We decided to go back the next day and see what the story was. Boy did we get a story!

It seems that about 30 years ago, Vashi the tailor, was drunk one night, like he was every night. His shop was failing, and he had little hope, even though one complete wall of his shop was totally taken up by an imposing and glittering god shelf, packed full of Indian idols. Even though he and his wife were in the shop practically 24 hours a day, the business just wasn't coming in. Well, they had just locked up for the night, having barely sold a thing all day and were thinking about starting back home. It was 11 PM.

As they made their way up the crowded street they saw this 'farang' (foreigner) walking by. Vashi's wife pushed her husband and said, "Go ask him if he wants a suit". Vashi resisted; after all, he was drunk, tired and wanted to go home, but his wife was insistent. He approached the man and slurred out an invitation to have a suit made. "Well, how about you show me what you've got," said the foreigner in a friendly way, so Vashi begrudgingly retraced his steps to the shop, pulled up the shutters and turned on the lights. The man looked around and then said, "Look, I'm leaving for the states in the morning, so I really don't have time for anything, but thanks anyway". Vashi then, understandably, got mad and said, "Why did you have me open the shop if you're not going to help me out? I've worked so hard but I still have no business and now you've done this to me!"

"Oh, sorry..." he smiled, "I'd be happy to pray for you!"

""Ha!" shouted Vashi. "Do you think I'm not doing that? Look at this enormous godshelf, it's doing NO good whatsoever." The foreigner smiled again and said, "Let's try the REAL GOD" and he bowed his head and prayed quietly. He then invited them to the church just a couple of blocks away and said that even though he'd be on a plane in the morning, he was sure they'd be welcome.

The next morning Vashi's wife said, "How about you just go and check out that church while I mind the shop... we certainly can use something that's real!" So even though he didn't particularly want to go, it was better than sitting around watching his business go down the drain, Vashi went to church for the first time... and the rest is history. Now 30+ years later, Vashi's tailor shop sits in the middle of the steaming red light district. They keep it there because YWAM missionaries use the storefront every night, all night long as a prayer and ministry oasis for the countless prostitutes that are searching for the truth.

...and Tony's getting a new suit, all because of a shy and quiet man who barely influenced OUR lives but acted on the voice of the Holy Spirit, leading him to impact thousands.

Remember to listen to that still small voice (not the pushy one that belongs to your wife) as you go thru this week and see what the Lord has in store for you.
Fondly,
Tony and Marsha

> *...because our gospel came to you not simply with words, but also with power, with the Holy Spirit and with deep conviction... (1Thessalonians 1:15)*

14. Does it Matter?
(October 4th)

I'm getting more confused. Today I asked in flawless Thai where there was an air conditioned cafe, followed their directions in Thai, found it, went in, sat down, wiped off some of the sweat and very politely... ordered a SKIRT! (It's that tone thing again; never mind).
We were visiting the world's largest (who's measuring?) outdoor market. I really don't like the place because as soon as you step 'in' you're lost. I had a list. I wanted to find seeds to grow some mint (OK, maybe I'm a little bit homesick) and maybe some fresh vegetables. Instead we walked thru millions of fish, dead, alive, or struggling. Then there were the deep fried bugs, a real treat for the gourmand, I'm told, the illegal endangered birds who aren't being taken care of well at all, and of course all the temple furnishings, tourist frip frap and enough jeans to cover all the legs in the world. Add to that so many people you can't believe it and about 110 degrees. You can see why my brain was addled.
I think we've been here about three months now. Our Thai is definitely better than when we arrived. It's easy to be 'better' when you start at ZERO. It's still so frustrating, though. I'm talking to anything that will move, using my limited vocabulary and grammar to say

things like "it how long?" or "me have no... uh, uh..." Of course Tony's much more reserved, so he's adapting the 'strong silent' look and only occasionally opens his mouth to pontificate something like "With Diarrhea like that you better cancel your holiday!" (Yes, he meant to say that. Didn't apply to anybody, but it's just so much fun to roll it off your tongue... the words, I mean).

On a happy note, we had coffee with our 'ruujack' (see the blog about kangaroos) from Hong Kong this week. We chatted away in Japanese for two hours and really felt 'at home'. So different from our normal day! She talked with tears in her eyes about being all alone for a year before we came, and how her son was sick and in the hospital and because she was new and knew no one, didn't know how to find a church that spoke Japanese... basically she had no one to turn to. Then she got the letter from me, saying that we'd arrived, she came to a Japanese concert that we invited her to, made some Christian friends who live in HER building and has now been to church as well as a Bible study on Wednesday! That day when she left I had a true feeling of actually MATTERING for the first time in a long time!

Hopefully, some day we can help make a difference to some Thai people as well. Only God knows. In the meantime they'll just get a chuckle out of me and move on.
Have a good week!
Tony and Marsha

> *You hear, O LORD, the desire of the afflicted; you encourage them, and you listen to their cry.*
> *(Psalms 10:17)*

15. Lost (?)
(October 11th)

I want to say a word or two about the word, "lost". We sometimes use it to describe death: "I lost my wife", "I lost a child", and in the same breath talk about losing our keys, our way, our train of thought, our sense of purpose. One word, but worlds of difference.

This week some dear dear friends 'lost' their baby, stillborn at 7 months.

But in the midst of our grief, we had to remember that he's NOT LOST! We all know exactly where he is, and he's WITH his heavenly Father.

What is truly lost is OUR experience with him. We were looking forward to knowing him and we feel robbed of that. We are lost to seeing his smile, hearing his little laugh and watching him bring his mommy a muddy frog or toddle off to school. We lost the chance for that prideful moment of watching him graduate from medical school having found the cure for the very thing that took him home this last week. That's where the real pain comes into play.

We stumbled around all this past week, "lost" in grief... staring at the walls, wishing we were there instead of here, shaking our fists at God and reminding Him that there is not a more deserving couple on the planet and asking WHY is this happening to them? No answer, just that "peace be still" sort of quietness.

The Thai word for death is sorta loosely translated as "the life force was unable to continue and so..." The Thais are a gentle people, but unfortunately 99% of them really are lost: lost to a dying world of sin. That's where we hope to make a difference someday.

Other than that, it's been a rather ordinary week. Marsha struggled with a case of food poisoning, spending a day or so curled up groaning, and as always, Tony feels a bit frustrated with his progress in acquiring language skills, (he's really doing fine, just needs more patience). But thanks be to God, I'm well now and will steer clear of that WESTERN STYLE bakery till they learn to wash their hands. Tony spent the day doing what he loves best, preaching, doing Lord's supper and having meetings, etc in the language he loves, Japanese. In his words, "It was like a day at Disneyland."

We have one week left with the private tutor, polishing up what we should know, and then next week (Oct 20th) we'll jump back into the foray of organized language school, this time to pick up reading and writing... pray for stamina and that we don't indeed LOSE our minds, which, of course IS a possibility!

Love ya,

Marsha

*All this is for your benefit, so that the grace that
is reaching more and more people may cause
thanksgiving to overflow to the glory of God. Therefore
we do not lose heart. Though outwardly we are wasting
away, yet inwardly we are being renewed day by day.
(2 Corinthians 4:15-16)*

16. A Quiet Week
(October 18th)

When the kids were little, we used to listen to cassette tapes of a guy named Garrison Keillor, who would tell stories in a quiet mid-American accent, reminiscing about rural life back in his hometown. This was probably my kids' only glimpse of the kind of life their parents had known when they were young. Garrison always started his monologues with the phrase, "Well, it's been a quiet week in Lake Woebegon."

It's also been a quiet week in "Lake Soi Attakawee" where we live. It's not usually a lake, but it sure has been most of this past week because of unseasonal rain, even for the rainy season. You should have seen us yesterday, heading out our driveway in water up to our knees, guitar and book bag wrapped in plastic bags, hoping to find a taxi driver brave enough to come down our canal/street! (I'll try to attach a picture).

We enjoyed our last week with the private tutor, trying to firm up the Thai that we have and getting ready to start learning to read and write with those funny looking chicken scratches they call an alphabet.

We've also enjoyed having a bit more time for Tony to focus on Japanese work. This weekend, he was the main speaker/singer for an event of about 40 Japanese who

get together every month to listen to a "special guest".
It was so exciting to see that many people who are beginning to realize that there IS a God and He might have a personal interest in them. Then today we went to a High Anglican Church with a British Vicar preaching, and every nationality imaginable present. We caught up with a lovely boy from Vietnam (I wrote about him and his family's plight as refugees last year, do you remember?), and then we all had lunch with some Australian friends. To top off the day we went to see a Thai love story at the movies.

Thanks for praying for us in advance as we head back to that "fire hydrant" of language learning we call formal language school. It starts Tuesday and hopefully in just 8 short weeks, it'll be over, and we'll be ready to well and truly start to work!

Hope your week was as "quiet" as ours. Have a great one coming up.

Love ya,

Tony and Marsha

He makes me lie down in green pastures, he leads me beside quiet waters… (Psalms. 23:2)

17. Lovin The Job
(October 25th)

Do any of you remember as a child reading your first word? For our boys, it was the "toto" brand on Japanese toilets. For Nicki, I think it was "kaka", only because Nathan would write it down and go to great pains to teach it to her, then roll over laughing when she'd try it out on us. For Tony and me, yesterday, it was the unabandoned joy of reading the word "YAA" in Thai letters and understanding that it meant "medicine". Never mind that it was written just over a huge sign in English which said "Pharmacy"; we would have gotten it; honest. We were so excited. I wish I could write it for you in Thai so you could be impressed, but my computer would probably blow up. Anyway, along with our first driving experience in Bangkok, it's been a real gold star week.

We've been thinking a lot about our "Work" lately, especially as we anticipate finishing our school requirement in a few months and start earning our keep. Also one of the comments in the blog: "WHY are you doing this to yourselves?" caused us to stop and consider, why indeed? It's no secret that we get really homesick some days, and it doesn't help that we've done the math, and find we COULD retire today if we really wanted to. But to do that would mean giving up the JOB, and that's a big step in anybody's book.

Just what is our "job" anyway, and what does it matter if we show up for work tomorrow or not? Oswald Chambers, our favorite devotional writer, has been talking a lot about "jobs" this last week. He seems to say over and over "Quit trying to "work for Jesus"; simply let Jesus reflect who He is THROUGH you and be what you are at the end of the day: His precious child. Now on one hand, I suppose that could be read as a proof text for why we should clean out our desk and head for home. But would that be reflecting Jesus through our lives? Today... I think not. I say that, because, well, as much as we groan and complain about our "tough" missionary lives (which I'll have to be honest with you, is not that bad), the simple fact is, we love what God is letting us do today.

I saw that reflected in Tony's eyes this morning, as he preached at another Japanese church. Yeah, it wasn't Thai, and I still had to beat him to make him do his homework tonight, but just watching him up there, telling the people how much God loves them, and praying that somehow they would know the joy of knowing the Savior, I had to admit, he LOVES what he's doing. And so do I. The only other place I've seen that kind of joy this week is in the faces of the employees at our local department store. These guys work 10 – 12 hour shifts for a wage that most of us would consider a travesty. Then every day at 5:00 PM, (after they're about half way through their shift) the whole store stops and sings the company song while the employees dance around the aisles. Yeah, it's silly, but they seem to love it. We make it a point sometimes to do our shopping around 5:00 just so we can catch the show. It's infectious; I hope the way our own joy is seen.

I'll try to load a couple of pictures of these guys on the blog. Make a note of the price checker on roller blades, now THAT might be fun! Are you loving your job? If not, why not? Want to talk about it?

Love,

Marsha

So I commend the enjoyment of life, because nothing is better for a man under the sun than to eat and drink and be glad. Then joy will accompany him in his work all the days of the life God has given him under the sun. (Ecclesiastes 8:15)

18. Green Wood Doesn't Burn Well
(November 1st)

The Thais must be a very clever people.

We've been studying 'reading and writing' for two weeks, and our brains are about fried. Language is such an interesting thing. Last night we went to see one of our missionary kids star in the high school play, "The Miracle Worker". Tony said he could really relate to Helen Keller, stumbling around bumping into walls, screaming and throwing tantrums because she wasn't understood. As you can recall, she just needed to COMMUNICATE!

One of the students in my class at language school laughs now that she's realized that during the first month of school, she kept going up to strangers and saying in Thai, "Hello, what's my name?" ...Oh how we can relate! Let me give you a little language lesson. Apparently consonants (all 44 of them) can appear anywhere in the word, you just work it out how they relate. Vowels (I think there are something like 24 or so) fit in BEFORE and AFTER, ABOVE and BELOW the consonant. Then of course you have the five tones, marked for the most part, above the word. CRAZY? You're right. I asked why there were FIVE separate letters for the sound TH and the teacher just said, "Ask the King who created the alphabet 500 years ago". I figure he was bored and didn't want anyone to be able to read. Mind you, if you use the WRONG letter for the sound 'TH" no one will understand it.

Then there's the spoken language which we've mentioned before. With five tones, you can say, for example, the word MAI, five different ways; down, falling, level, rising and high, thus enabling you to say, using ONLY the word, "MAI", great sentences like "Green wood doesn't burn well does it?" Very handy.

Let me tell you a story about "MAI". Every day we stop and buy fruit from a vendor with a little sidewalk cart on our walk home from school. For about 75 cents, he gives us 1/2 lb of fresh fruit in a plastic bag, all cut up and ready to eat. Now the Thais like to walk along and eat this fruit, using a wooden skewer that the vendor kindly sticks in the sack. We find these wooden sticks of no value, because we bring the fruit home and put it in a bowl. The skewer is called... you guessed it: a "MAI". But it's the MAI that goes waaaayyyyy up in tone, like you're saying MAAAIII?????

Ok. So we don't want the sticks, and in order to say, "No thank you, I must say... wait for it... "MAI OW", only this time the MAI is a falling tone, like the Doppler effect you'd hear from someone falling off a cliff.

I say, "MAI Ow", but accidently, in my excitement say MAAAI??? OW...... which means, "I WANT STICKS!"

He nods and adds a couple more to the sack. I shout louder (this will help?) I WANT STICKS!! So I get more and more as I shout louder and louder. We walk away with a sack of fruit and 15 sticks. Guess he thought we were going to walk along with a crowd while we were munching on our fruit.

I'm going to have to work on my tones. Maybe tomorrow I can say, "I do not require the addition of those annoying little wooden objects"... or something. Have a great week, and don't just shout louder when you're misunderstood!

Love ya,

Marsha

They said, "All right, say 'Shibboleth'". If he said, "Sibboleth", because he could not pronounce the word correctly, they seized him and killed him at the fords of the Jordan. Forty-two thousand Ephraimites were killed at that time. (Judges 12:6)

19. Floating Our Boat
(November 8th)

This week we experienced one of Thailand's huge festivals known as "Loy Krathong", which roughly translated I think means something like "Float Your Boat". According to what we can work out with our limited Thai, it began about a thousand years ago, when someone made a "krathong", or a basket out of banana leaves, and put in it all of their bad feelings and 'sins', lit a candle on it and floated it away on the river. A beautiful image, when you think about it, and one which no one in our line of work would want to miss.

Of course, we didn't go to the river to float away our sins. In fact, we didn't even go to the river. As it turned out, there were a few hundred thousand folks who opted to go instead to our very own shopping area, where there's an adjoining park with a beautiful meandering pond running through it. Not exactly your "sins down the river" type venue, but just the ticket for those of us who were more interested in the party atmosphere than the deeper spiritual meaning. Lots of families turned out, and it was refreshing to see them truly enjoying the night, taking pictures, lighting fireworks and launching their not-so-sturdy crafts into the waiting jaws of the huge carp who lurk just under the surface. Most of the boats were made of bread, so it was a real feast all around. Pity the poor pond, which I think will take until this time next year to recover!

We met a LOT of kimono-clad Japanese in the park, which is not surprising, since the whole festival looks and feels a lot like "Obon", a summer festival back in Japan when you pay respect to your ancestors while at the same time get in some serious party-making. We even found a family from Sendai, our hometown for 20 years. It was so good talking to them and inviting them to church. I do so hope we'll see them again.

So it was a good evening, even though both Loy Krathong and Obon are kind of sad, when you think about it. Just imagine having no reasonable way to deal with your sin and grief except to chuk some bread into the river and hope for the best. We listened to a Thai pastor last Sunday who shared a real gem. He said, "Whenever people ask me, 'Can a Christian participate in Loy Krathong?' I tell them, 'Absolutely! And when you make your boat, make sure you top it off with a little cross right in the center. When you release it into the water, tell the people around you, THAT'S where my sin and sorrow is going: as far as the east is from the west, thanks to the cross of Jesus!'"

We're already making plans for next year's celebrations. Anybody got some ideas for a waterproof bread boat

topped with a cross?
Love ya,
Marsha

The next day John saw Jesus coming toward him and said, "Look, the Lamb of God, who takes away the sin of the world!" (John 1:29)

20. A Final Word About Language
(November 15th)

In couple of days we'll be finished with our classroom studies. Then the real work starts, as we try to hone what we've learned with a private tutor so that we can pass the mission's "Level Three Assessment". This will indicate to them that we're safe to turn loose on the street and they won't have to come rescue us. We will then be free to get to the work that we came to do, most likely with Japanese. Our goal is have it all done and dusted by Christmas.

I know you've all heard me complaining, but those of you who know me, know that I love a challenge. Tony and I have worked harder on this language thing than anything we've done since... well, I guess since we learned Japanese 30 years ago. I think it's been doubly hard this time because it seems that we're working with half the brain cells we once had. It HAS given us a greater appreciation for the Japanese language, though, because when we have a chance to speak it here, it comes SO MUCH EASIER than the Thai we're struggling with... and we can't even remember ever having learned it! Isn't it amazing how time heals?

Anyway, I thought I'd give you one more bit of insight into this whole language thing, after which I promise to put the books away and start focusing on other issues at hand.

Did you know... that Thai WOULD be one of the world's hardest languages, (along with Japanese) but some king back 500 years ago had the sense to snatch some Sanskrit letters and make an alphabet instead of the pictographs that haunt the Japanese and Chinese? HOWEVER, because Thai doesn't have quite as many different words as some languages, but still has the desire to say a lot of stuff, they've interjected FIVE tones into the words they have. This is a handy trick that turns one sound into... five different words, depending on the tone. (Remember my previous blog about green wood burning?) You can get a lot more words for your money this way! So, (here's the trick) in order to enable you to read the sound with the proper tone, they use a different letter to say the same sound, depending on its TONE (you lost yet?) This week we've struggled with learning all the rules for the 44 various letters, (this one goes UP when you say it, that one is flat, etc). I was doing pretty good until they added some NEW rules that changed everything. It was not a good day! Now we realize that, for example, if the "N" has an "H" in front of it, then we (somehow), know that the sound "H" is not pronounced, but it makes the "N" sound now go DOWN instead of UP. AAAAKKK. Apparently Thais learn this with no personal pain at about age seven or eight! Let me be illiterate! I can imagine you're tired just trying to understand what I'm saying, so you can just imagine taking dictation!

But wait, even if I can't read, and believe me, I can't, I reckon I'll be hit by the train by the time I work out the "Don't" word. Just in speaking, though, there're all those CLASSIFIERS! Maybe we have them in English as well... (do we?). Do we say, "Give me two glasses of water?" I guess we do. WHEN did we learn that? Whoever thought you'd have to indicate HOW you want your water? Ok. So I'll admit the English language has classifiers, but I think they at least make sense. Listen to some of these classifiers: A "tua" is a counter for a body. (One body, two bodies, etc). Fair enough, but did you know a camera is a "tua"? That's because when cameras first were introduced, they had tripods, and those are legs... and... you're following the thinking, right? BODIES have legs, cameras have legs... How about "gawn", the classifier for sugar, cakes and BATTERIES? (I always think of those things together!) Of course there are pairs, but not for eyeglasses or trousers, because they are never apart, so you don't need to infer a 'pair', but "twins" are just a "people pair", fair enough. I think it's cute that the classifier for Boat and Airplane are the same, because when the Thais saw the first airplane, they could only conceptualize it as a 'flying boat'!

Well, hopefully next week when you read the blog, we'll be somewhat recovered from the daily grind of the commute to the language school and will be enjoying the tutor instead.

Now we're off to the neighbors who can't speak English either, but they're lovely FRENCH missionaries, here looking for a place to set up work. They've offered to serve us a real French meal, so we're excited. Tony can still remember how to say "Where is the post office?" from his college French class, so we're looking forward to a riveting evening.

Bon Appetite'

Marsha

...but no man can tame the tongue. It is a restless evil, full of deadly poison. (James 3:8)

21. Got the Bubble?
(November 22nd)

The other day as I was pouring myself a glass of water from our kitchen dispenser (you CAN drink the water in Bangkok, but only at your peril), I was startled by a loud gurgling sound, followed by silence... a sure sign that it was time to lug a new water jug into the house. The sound took me back to a faint childhood memory, sitting around the table while Mom poured Dad a cup of coffee. Suddenly a tiny burp came from the spout, and then Dad's coffee was being filled with that muddy sediment from the bottom of the pot.

"Uh oh," she said, "Looks like you got the bubble." And from then on, the phrase took on a whole world of applications, all related to the fact that whatever we were doing, or pouring or saying, was just about to come to an end. "Getting the bubble" meant the last dregs were being drained out, and there was no more to come.

Now, I don't have to be much of a preacher to see the obvious application here, as well as draw myself up to Brother Paul's observation that he was "already being poured out like a drink offering, and the time has come for my departure." (2 Timothy 4:6)

I heard a guy one time say, "If my life is indeed being poured out, then I figure by now I should be about half used up." Ain't that a fact! What more terrible tragedy than to find ourselves arriving at the throne of God with energy unspent, strength unused, potential untapped? No, I think I want to get to Heaven and say, "Here I am, Lord; I'm totally drained. My life has been poured out, right to the bubble."

Now don't misunderstand me here; I'm not saying that my "bubble" has come, and I'm ready to hang up my spurs. I think (dare I say "hope"?) I still have a few good cuppas left in me. I'm not so sure about a Japanese pastor I visited with this last week. After several bypass surgeries, throat surgery and about 80 laps around the sun, this old gentleman is giving it a 101% just to stand up and preach on Sunday. But he's doing just that, and he has my profound respect. And when his "bubble" does come, I can imagine him being lifted up to the Throne and God saying to him, "Well done; you've poured out every last drop for the sake of my Kingdom. Now come on inside and enjoy what I've prepared for you."

You feeling "poured out" today? Good on ya! What was that old Folgers coffee commercial? "Good to the last drop." That's what I want, and that's my prayer for each of you.

But even if I am being poured out like a drink offering on the sacrifice and service coming from your faith, I am glad and rejoice with all of you. (Philippians. 2:17)

22. Hark Now Hear
(November 29th)

Well, when you get this blog a lot of you have survived, with joy I hope, another Thanksgiving. It was a good day for us, too, thanks to a cooperative effort on the part of our mission. Everybody brought food, someone found a turkey, and it was a feast! It was fun to be with so many new faces and realize that we all have so much to be thankful for.

Also, as we are technically living in the northern hemisphere, we too, are enjoying the 'fall' weather. For a few days now it's been below 90 degrees (30 C) and so 'refreshing' as to inspire us to take long walks. We always walk since we don't have a car, but this time we're enjoying it a bit more than usual. It's funny to see some of the more loved dogs wearing sweaters because of the perceived cold!

Now we can all move into the Christmas season! Believe it or not, it's really BIG here in Thailand. Of course, not for any of the right reasons.

I may have said this before, but we believe the Thai people ARE really quite religious. They're just religious about the wrong thing.

Yesterday we walked by one of the largest shrines in the city. It's dedicated to "Erawan" which, as Google will tell you, is a three headed mythical Hindu elephant... and I love this part, "born of Khun Lek Viriyapant's ideas and imagination". If that doesn't say it all... Anyway, it seems that every day literally thousands of people stop by this corner in downtown Bangkok in their busy lives to pray. For more money, the girls in the background will get up and dance to achieve more clout, I suppose. From the overhead walkway where we were watching from, thousands more Thais 'wai" (bow with their hands together in the famous Thai greeting) to the shrine as they hurry past in their busy days.

The oxymoron yesterday was that while all this was going on as it does every day of the year... there was some rather loud Christmas music playing along the walkway. Not your 'jingle bells' type Christmas noise that is becoming more and more politically correct in western countries, but actual CHRISTIAN Christmas music!

Anyway, try to imagine hundreds of people bowing and praying... to an imaginary three headed elephant. It's so sad. But even sadder was that as we stood there listening to the music, a well dressed businessman came up to the shrine, bought some incense sticks, and fell to his knees before the elephant altar. Not only did he "wai" in traditional fashion, he went all the way to the ground, beating his head with his hands, as if desperately trying to make his prayers heard. What was he praying for? I guess we'll never know, but the real tragedy was that in the midst of his prayer, the speakers behind us were blaring out the poignant words to "Mary's boy child... hark now hear the angels sing". My heart broke for the Thai people, so ambitious, so searching... so lost.

And you see and hear how this fellow Paul has convinced and led astray large numbers of people here in Ephesus and in practically the whole province of Asia. He says that man-made gods are no gods at all.
(Acts 19:26)

23. A Fine and Beautiful Thing
(December 6th)

You might remember Tony wrote a blog a couple of weeks ago about "pouring out your life for the Lord"... Well, Tony was sick this last week. I mean a sickness of biblical proportions. People worried that it was the swine flu, and it might have been, but he got better instead of worse. Albeit it said, as he was pouring out his life and losing 7 lbs, (3 kilos for the metric bunch) we were thankful to have indoor plumbing!

Now he's better and trying NOT to find the 7 lbs again, but I'm sure they're going to find him as he is eating again... And that reminds me of a little story.

Years ago I was a young missionary in Japan. I was there to save the world, and maybe just a tad filled with myself. One night I went alone to the evening service at church. Tony must have had a meeting somewhere or was at home with the kids, I don't remember.

Anyway, I was sitting there, the only foreigner in the service. The text for the message was Matthew, where the lady is pouring out perfume on the Master's feet.

Pastor Noguchi read the passage and then talked a few minutes about the woman, the cost of the perfume, etc. You've heard this sermon before. Then he took an interesting turn and said, "Look at our missionaries". I was glad I was paying attention as all eyes focused on me.

He continued. "They are obviously leaders back home where they come from. They are talented and intelligent. They would have to have drive and ambition or they wouldn't have made it this far," he continued. I sat up in my seat and beamed with pride. Then he said, somewhat to my surprise...

"And they get here, and what? They study the language for a very long time, and all they can achieve is to talk like 6 yr olds. They never really understand us, and they are bumbling around lost most of the time". (I shrank in my seat as my face turned red. I knew he was right) There was some murmuring and nodding in agreement. Noguchi went on, "Sometimes we might be tempted to just thank these folks, and kindly suggest that they go back home where they can do some real work; where they will be comfortable and can really use their skills?" After a brief pause, before everyone started voting us off the island, he picked up his Bible and read the words of Jesus, this time in SIMPLE ENGLISH. "Forbid her not, for what she does is a fine and beautiful thing".

"Don't you see?" he said to the congregation. "Missionaries all over the world are pouring out their LIVES at the feet of Jesus... for whatever it's worth, what they are doing is a Fine and Beautiful thing!"

That was a turning point in my life when I realized I'll never be Japanese (or Thai). I will never speak any language like a native, including American English, which seems like such a long time ago, and Australian, which my Aussie brothers and sisters insist IS English. But like it or not, my life IS being poured out, as the wrinkles on my face confirm. What a comfort to think that Jesus might give me a squeeze and say, "Good on ya, Marsha!"

In all truth, it's not much of a sacrifice to love these people, and if that's part of what "pouring out" means, then I can't complain. I guess the bottom line is simply this: our lives are running out, at least the part associated with our mortal bodies. The question is not, "How can I plug the leak?" but, "How can my pouring out make a difference to the Kingdom?"

May your pouring be a good one, and may it be said that it was indeed a fine and beautiful thing.

Love ya,

Marsha

When she poured this perfume on my body, she did it to prepare me for burial. I tell you the truth, wherever this gospel is preached throughout the world, what she has done will also be told, in memory of her.

(Matthew 26:12 – 13)

24. News From Camp
(December 13th)

I'm writing today from camp. We're up in the mountains about three hours from Bangkok with 60 enthusiastic Thai young adults and 15 very energetic Australians! The Aussies, from Brisbane's Kenmore Baptist Church, come every year and do an English camp for the student centre kids and they just keep getting better.

Anyway, it's been a crazy couple of days, what with wild games, boisterous singing, and even a Thai rendition of an Australian bush dance (Hey you Aussies, is there really such a dance as "The Waves of Bondi, or are they making this stuff up?").

It's also nice to be a bit cooler than usual, thanks to the camp's location, up in the mountains. The place is beautiful, the food is... well, interesting, and the beds are reminiscent of an English torture rack, but hey, it's camp! But I think the thing I'll remember most are the testimonies we're hearing. The Aussies have honed their stories down to simple English, free of all the cultural and religious trappings, and the kids are really being blessed by hearing them.

Even more important are the testimonies of some of the Thais themselves who have found Christ. Often thru studying English, they've come to understand the deeper meanings that go so much farther than the words they struggled with. We've seen firsthand this weekend that issues like forgiveness, mercy and love are just as much a part of the Thai people as they are in our own histories. What a miracle, that God can make the Bible's words fresh and relevant to any language, anytime!

You might remember I wrote awhile back about the refugee boy who is a part of the student centre program. He's still here. The USA did not grant them admission, even though he and his family of six brothers and sisters, plus Mum and Dad are officially recognized as refugees. The Mrs helped the Americans in years past, and their government is still trying to catch her and punish her again... But with the help of some great people from Kenmore, they applied to Australia, and have been accepted, but now the Thai government won't let them go, because of some unspoken agreement with the other country. Please continue to pray for them. I can't imagine living your whole life afraid of being found by assassins (The family has had to move twice this past year when it looked like they'd been spotted. Mum never leaves the single room they live in, and the kids only go out to go to a local school and attend church). Even though that is their lot, the son who's here at camp continues to talk about God's goodness and BOUNTY.

I don't know about you, but when I go to bed tonight,

I'm going to say a special prayer of thanks for God's protection, and for the often taken-for-granted blessing of peace and security in a world where it's so often hard to find.

This time next week, Tony and I will be on the plane for Australia!! I can't believe it's been a whole year since we've seen our baby girl. (Who's really 20, but she's still our baby. And while it's a little early to meet our first and only Grandchild (appearance scheduled for February), at least we'll be able to share a few days with the proud parents-to-be. Stay tuned!

Love ya,

Marsha

I lift up my eyes to the hills— where does my help come from? My help comes from the LORD, the Maker of heaven and earth. (Psalms 121:1 – 2)

25. Semantics or Relationship?
(December 20th)

Today marks the end of a long and arduous lifetime of (only??) five months of language school. We are not done learning, but we are hoping for permission to get to the reason we came here, and that's the Japanese. All that will hopefully be decided in January.

I heard an interesting thing this last week. Our friend was interviewing Thai people to work in the Baptist student center. A middle-aged lady came in, and sat stiffly across from him as he looked over her application. In the box marked "Religion" she had written "Buddhist". James thought it was interesting that she would be applying to work in a Christian institution, but figured this was another one of those "who can understand the Thai" issues, continued to the next page where the questions got deeper. "Who is Jesus Christ?" She answered, "My Lord and Saviour," "Why do you believe that Jesus Died on the Cross". Answer, "For my sins". The questions continued in the same vein.

James became a bit confused so he laid down the application and said, "You say you're Buddhist but you're answering as a Christian, what's up?"

She smiled and answered back confidently. "Of course I'm Buddhist, I'm THAI, but I believe that Jesus is the son of God who died for my sins and I have asked him to be lord of my life. My family has known for years that I'm different and some of them have even started believing in Jesus as well.

Semantics. James explained that being a Christian is a RELATIONSHIP, not a nationality!

She got big tears in her eyes and took the application. She turned it over to the first page and marked out "Buddhist" and wrote in big bold letters, "CHRISTIAN!"

This Christmas season I hope we all know both our nationality and our relationship to the Savior!

On a personal note, we fly to our little ducklings in Australia tonight at nine. We're flying that pinnacle of cheap airlines, "Jetstar" so please pray that it stays aloft all thru the night! We'll be there almost two weeks and can hardly wait. I don't think mothers were meant to be away from their babies, especially the still growing up daughters for a year at a time...

Merry Christmas to all!!!

Marsha and Tony

My purpose is that they may be encouraged in heart and united in love, so that they may have the full riches of complete understanding, in order that they may know the mystery of God, namely, Christ.
(Colossians 2:2)

26. Merry Christmas Happy New Year!

(December 27th)

Greetings from Down Under! It's our first Sunday in Australia and Tony is getting ready to preach at our home church in Gold Coast this morning.

We've had a great Christmas, visiting with Nathan and Kylie in their new apartment in Sydney. Some of you out there will know what it's like to feel an unborn baby move. Kylie was quite gracious to provide us constant entertainment, as we watched and felt the antics of little Baby Woods (nobody knows yet whether it's a boy or girl; we'll all be surprised in February!) Only 6 weeks to go and our first grandchild will be here. It certainly gives us pause to realize that time is marching on.

We're enjoying catching up with old friends, most of whom we haven't seen for over 18 months. Even our own daughter Nicki has changed (for the good) in a year. It's been special to catch up with all her great adventures.

We'll let you go today, I know you're all full and busy as you tidy up 2009 and look forward to 2010!

Love ya,
Marsha

"Before I formed you in the womb I knew you, before you were born I set you apart; I appointed you as a prophet to the nations." (Jeremiah 1:5)

27. Here's one from down under
(January 3rd)

How time flies, can you believe it's 2010 already! Tony and I have had a GREAT GREAT 10 days here in our adopted home, Australia. It's been so good, I admit it's going to be a little tough getting on that plane tonight and head back to Thailand.

One of the big questions that we've heard a lot this week has been, "So how do you like Bangkok?" And the simple answer is, "We LOVE it... but sometimes we don't like it." I love the work we do, but it's hard to hold that up against spending Christmas with my kids.

And then I find myself coming back to the old familiar question. "What would Jesus do?" I wonder how much He loved dragging around in that all too vulnerable body, missing His own "home", but staying the course, just for us.

If it wasn't for the 80,000 Japanese in Bangkok without enough shepherds; if it wasn't for the honest and sweet answer we got from a Japanese couple just before we left last week who told us, "We've never in our lives thought about a personal relationship with a Savior"... believe me, we'd give up the adventure and GET HOME and rock the soon to be born grandbaby.

Please say a special prayer for us as we plough back

into it. By the time you get the next blog, we (hopefully) will be back home, will be losing all this Christmas fat and be in Chiang Mai visiting a Japanese church there. More news to come...
All the best for 2010! We love you all!
Marsha

And we know that in all things God works for the good of those who love him, who have been called according to his purpose. (Romans 8:28)

28. Bearing One Another's Burdens
(January 10th)

Tony here. I'm going to try and slip in this week's blog, since Marsha is enjoying a visit from her sister. If you're reading this, then I managed to convince her to take a break for one week and let me have a go!

And besides, I want to share a couple of prayer requests with you. It's been such an encouragement to hear your responses to Marsha's weekly submissions, and to know that we really ARE part of a larger family, working for the Kingdom and bearing one another up.

One of our Japanese groups here in Bangkok has been chopped off at the knees over the holidays. Kondo Sensei, the elderly pastor with heart and throat problems is now facing the added challenge of helping his wife through chemotherapy for lung cancer. They have to go back to Japan for that, and even though he says they will continue the work here, I see some difficult days ahead for them. If that's not bad enough, the church's main lay leader, Mr. Kitajima, was suddenly transferred back to Japan, effective next week. And then to top it off, the hotel where the group of 30-40 meet each week is going through renovations and has told them they must find another place from week after next.

I'm going to meet with some of the folks there next week

to discuss what we might be able to do, but first I have to go up to Chiangmai tomorrow to meet with another group of Japanese Christians whose pastor must retire soon. They're asking me to come help out, and although I don't think I should take on a full time pastor's role, I do hope I'll be able to help them come up with some kind of "roster" plan.

So all in all, things are shaping up to be an exciting time! I'll be honest with you: I'm trying my best to keep up with Thai language study, but with opportunities like these at my doorstep, it's hard to prioritize.

Marsha has long since passed me up with her studies, and I can see her pulling away on the horizon... which is a good thing, because SOMEBODY has to be able to keep bringing people like Blue and her Dad along in the faith (see earlier blog).

So please pray: for Kondo Sensei and his wife, for the flock under his care, for the Japanese Christians in Chiangmai, and for Marsha and I as we struggle to stay focused on what GOD wants of us here. I tell ya, I don't know what we'd do without family like you! God bless.

Is any one of you in trouble? He should pray. Is anyone happy? Let him sing songs of praise. Is any one of you sick? He should call the elders of the church to pray over him and anoint him with oil in the name of the Lord. (James 5:13 – 14)

29. A Bit of Encouragement
(January 18th)

We're a bit late getting this posted this week. Let me explain.

You will remember that we spent Christmas with our kids and friends in Australia. It was a better visit than we could have dreamed of and went entirely too fast.

Then Christmas was over and we came back to Thailand fat and happy but with a palatable sense of discouragement. After all, while we were gone, nothing changed here. The Thai are still wonderful but very lost and they haven't improved their language so that we can understand it any better! The temperatures are still in the 90's even though it's winter and most importantly Tony turns 62 this month so naturally... the question 'why are we doing this?' was eating pretty heavily at us.

I prayed for some encouragement as we ploughed back into language study and work... not really expecting an answer. I think it was more of a rhetorical, "help", but boy was I surprised!

We had been asked to go up to Chiang Mai and meet with the Japanese up there (several hundred miles north of Bangkok, where the second largest population of Japanese are). The meeting was amazing and hopefully we can go back on a regular basis and help the one pastor minister to the four or five thousand that are there. While we were there we helped with the devotions at the missionary kid dormitory. The dorm parent there now, was a missionary kid in a dorm WE ran in Liberia about 32 years ago. That was encouraging too, to see how God's plan has worked out in him over the years... but here's the unexpected, unexplainable surprise.

While we were there, we got a notification from our mission that we'd been given some money designated for our ministry to Japanese.

Now, you're probably thinking "so what?" After all, we're missionaries, that's how we operate. However, if you know US, you'll know that almost NOBODY ever gives us money. It's almost a joke with Tony's dad, who as a retired missionary, gets honorariums every time he speaks, whereas we get asked to pay the utilities since the church service ran late! To add to the intrigue, this money came from someone we don't know.

Well, we checked it out, and it wasn't easy, but we discovered that the gift is from a gentleman in Tennessee (our home is Colorado) who, although he isn't even a Baptist, 'heard' of us and sent it... BECAUSE WE'RE WORKING WITH JAPANESE IN THAILAND!

Call me silly, but what a creative way for God to say to two old discouraged missionaries who'd mostly rather be home with the grandbaby (due next month!)... "This is MY way, walk in it!"

All of this happened last week and the last few days have been full of encouragement and opportunity. That's part of the reason this blog is late, we've been meeting with Japanese leaders, getting more and more opportunities to do ministry, talking and actually being understood by Thais, hitting the language study again... if we keep this up, we'll be 65 by the time we take the next breath!

Hope you all have blessed weeks as well. It's fun when you can see God's involvement!

Till next week, Tony and Marsha

The people of Israel, including the Levites, are to bring their contributions of grain, new wine and oil to the storerooms where the articles for the sanctuary are kept and where the ministering priests, the gatekeepers and the singers stay. "We will not neglect the house of our God." (Nehemiah 10:39)

30. Crisis and opportunity
(January 24th)

Well, it's been a great week. Tony's finally getting up to speed with the Japanese work, with ALMOST more opportunities to minister than he can handle! As of now, we have active work going on with three groups here in Bangkok, one in the town of Chiang Mai (an hour's flight north), and one down in Chon Buri (two hour's drive south). Kondo Sensei, the pastor we mentioned before, has gone back to Japan to help his wife through another round of chemo, and while they're away, Tony will be heading up that group, not only preaching but trying to help them prepare for a rather uncertain future. I thought the point he made on Sunday was one we might all take to heart ourselves. Let me see if I can share it with you: The Japanese word, "Kiken" means "danger", and it's made up of two characters: "ki" and "ken". There's another word for "opportunity", and that's the word, "kikai". It's also made up of two characters, "ki" (not the same as the one for danger) and "kai". Now here's why we love this language: If you take the first character of "kiken", danger, and combine it with the first character of "kikai", "opportunity", you have a whole new word, pronounced (can you guess?) "Kiki". And it means... "crisis": a time of danger; a time of opportunity.

Tony's point for the struggling Japanese group on Sunday was simply put: Crisis is a part of life. It's not something to be avoided, but rather to be experienced, while looking closely for the opportunity it presents. When I think about it, some of the most significant experiences in my life have come about through crisis. What about you? I'd love to hear about how God has led you through the fires and brought you out the other side, a little better than you were before.

The first crisis a person meets is the crisis of birth. Just think of it: all of a sudden, that baby's life is turned literally upside down. He's thrust into a strange new world of sound and light and color. Strange hands are grasping him, slapping him, cutting him. Is it any wonder the newborn cries? And yet if you're reading this, then you did survive that first crisis. And I wonder, now that you look back on it, if you had a choice, would you rather have stayed in that nice, quiet, dark place, or would you choose to face the crisis and see what happens?

I can't help but think of my first grandchild, who now waits in that quiet comfortable place. What's going through his or her mind right now? Will he or she be ready for the crisis to come? Stay tuned!

PS, if you'd like to comment, and haven't yet figured out the mysteries of blogging, just send me an email. I'll put your thoughts into the blog myself, and we can all share them together.

Marsha

I have been constantly on the move. I have been in danger from rivers, in danger from bandits, in danger from my own countrymen, in danger from Gentiles; in danger in the city, in danger in the country, in danger at sea; and in danger from false brothers. I have labored and toiled and have often gone without sleep; I have known hunger and thirst and have often gone without food; I have been cold and naked. Besides everything else, I face daily the pressure of my concern for all the churches.
(2 Corinthians 11:26 – 28)

31. Keeping up with old friends
(January 31st)

Yesterday was Tony's 62nd birthday. I think that's a significant one because people tell us we can now start drawing Social Security!
Honestly, I'd rather someone tell us we qualify for a college grant or a baby bonus. I always thought people on Social Security were OLD! But then, now that I look at it, it's more like, "Cool! Money from the government? Let it come, because I can sure think of some ways to enjoy it!"
Fortunately we still have our minds (at least that's what my mind is telling me!), and yesterday we met some new missionaries here and in the process found a long lost friend. I think our paths wandered away from each other back in the 90's. In the mission world, losing a friend is a tough one, because that friend could be anywhere on the planet by now. However, when these new folks mentioned that they'd served in Austria, I found myself saying, "Do you know Charlie Brown"? They do, and now we know that our long lost friend with such an unforgettable name is in Mesquite Texas, near where we just spent six months last year on Furlough. How sad that we didn't know they were there till now.
Even sadder is when I realize that I can 'wander away'

from the friendship and relationship with our Lord from time to time. He too has an unforgettable name, but He doesn't move to some distant place... sadly, we're the ones wandering off......

I love the internet; I love the age we live in (at least most days) but isn't it wonderful that God is always just a thought away. He doesn't crash, or manage to get himself off the grid and lost... we live each day in His presence and blessing.

My prayer is that we don't get too busy or distracted to remember to keep up with our best friend, God, and I also hope we don't lose any of you either.

You all have a good week. We're busy busy; lots of new ministry happening. For example after Tony led the whole service in Japanese today and delivered the sermon, we went and did games and singing and playing with about 150 slum kids all afternoon. It was fun but on one hand daunting, when you realize how much more needs to be done to show these kids the love of Christ. However, it also makes you thankful that we're old enough to take the pace and survive!

Tony and Marsha, soon to be GRANDPARENTS! (talk about OLD!)

"I the LORD do not change. So you, O descendants of Jacob, are not destroyed. (Malachi 3:6)

32. Grandparents
(February 7th)

Well, as a lot of you know by now, we're GRANDPARENTS! With any luck, there'll be some pictures posted on our "meet the Woods" section of this blog.

I wondered how I'd feel... and I guess I'm still wondering, mostly because I haven't had the chance yet to hold him. I know I'll be ecstatic when it's real. A lady we were talking to this last week made the comment, "If I had known grandkids were so much fun, I'd have had them FIRST!"

They named him Isaac Trevor. Because they hadn't opted to know ahead of time whether he was a boy or girl, we hadn't spent much time contemplating names, and so this came as a compete surprise. But I have to admit it's a name we're totally thrilled with and had even secretly prayed for. Isaac, as you know, was the much anticipated and desired son of Abraham and his wife Sarah. Isaac means "laughter", and it was a natural for them, since that was Sarah's first response at hearing the news of the blessed event. And of course that's where the comparison has to stop, because Kylie is certainly not 80 years old (although she may feel that way in the next few weeks)!

As for the name, Trevor... again, a lot of you know that's the name of Nathan's older brother, who died at 16 of leukemia. How precious was our 'treasure' in Trevor, and now we can enjoy all of that again through Isaac. I had often wondered how Trevor and Nathan really felt about each other as they were six years apart. But right before he died, we took Trevor in a wheelchair to a boy scout meeting of Nathan's. I'll never forget Trevor looking across the room and saying, "You know, of all the guys in the room, Nathan's absolutely the coolest!". What an honor for two boys to have that kind of respect for each other even though on most days they squabbled with the best. Now Nathan has honored his brother by using his name. We're so proud.

And of course we're proud of little Isaac. Apparently he was born without putting Mom out too much, (five hours!) and in the first 48 hours has been... well, perfect. What can we say!

Meanwhile back at the ranch, Tony and I have to hit the Thai language extra hard, in spite of a tidal wave of new opportunities for ministry among the Japanese. This week, we've agreed to "interim" at a Japanese church in Chiang Mai starting in May and staying anywhere from one to five months. We've also managed to help a church here in Bangkok make a move from the hotel they've had to leave into a meeting room at our own Baptist mission offices, right next door to Calvary Baptist Church. Do I see a wedding on the horizon? And to top it off, we got a copy of "Fireproof" in Japanese (Great movie for couples who want to strengthen their marriage), as well as a Japanese study book to go with it. We "Beta tested" it with a Japanese couple yesterday, and they're ready to help us get a group going as soon as possible. Life's exciting!

Here's your homework, if you should choose... Tony, Marsha and Nicki are looking for names to present to Baby Isaac as possible handles. "Grandma, Grandpa and Aunt Nicki" just seem too boring! Any ideas?

Love ya,

Marsha

> "...the Angel who has delivered me from all harm — may he bless these boys. May they be called by my name and the names of my fathers Abraham and Isaac, and may they increase greatly upon the earth."
> *(Genesis 48:16)*

33. Body Language
(February 14th)

Thanks so much for all your congrats on our first little perfect grandson! We'll be seeing him this next Thursday, so IF I can put him down long enough to blog next week, you can guess what it'll be about!

This week, we saw something interesting while riding the train. Ordinarily there is a teeny little sign above some of the seats on the train that say, "Please give this seat to a monk".

Well, a monk got on the train and headed toward the middle of the car. Almost immediately, somebody JUMPED up and offered him a seat. Then the 'dance' began. As the monk sat down, the people on either side also exploded out of their seats up as if there were springs underneath them, now giving the monk THREE seats on a crowded train.

Then at the next stop, some guy with more nerve than me (I don't think he was Thai), sat down next to the monk, completely ignoring him but still leaving an empty seat on the other side of the holy man.

At the next stop, a lady carrying a baby got on. The guy who didn't mind sitting next to a monk got up and offered her his seat. She smiled and sat down.

Now it was the monk's turn. He SHOT up out of his seat

and stood till the next stop.

So you say, "Women trump Monks?" Who knows?

I thought about our body language and how it reflects what we believe inside. Thai people are deeply religious, or at least deeply superstitious, and NOBODY wants to be caught touching a monk. We were told when we first got here to avoid all physical contact, out of respect. If a woman ever wanted to give anything to a monk, she would have to lay it down in front of him, or else give it to his helper, so as to avoid the possibility for contact. But giving up your seat to a monk probably gives you merit with the Powers that be, or at least they think so.

Where do we stand with our 'body language'? Tony remembers back in Australia one morning as he was out for his daily walk/jog/pray time. As he was praying that morning, he discovered that he had unconsciously moved over so that Jesus would be on the street side, in the protective role. Tony chuckled to himself when he realized what he'd done, but later had to admit, when you LIVE your beliefs, they come out in your actions.

What is your body language saying this week?

He said to them: "You are well aware that it is against our law for a Jew to associate with a Gentile or visit him. But God has shown me that I should not call any man impure or unclean. (Acts 10:28)

34. Something To Celebrate
(February 21st)

As this has been an eventful week, I, Nicki Woods, their daughter, am writing the blog for them as they are currently away from the internet for a few days. Wish me luck. Psalms 39:5 says, You have made my days a mere handbreadth. What a week this has been! With the excitement of coming down to Sydney to see my parents, I can only image how much more overjoyed they are, seeing not just me but my brother Nathan, his wife Kylie AND their brand new baby, Isaac Trevor Woods. The occasion called for two celebrations: the birth of their first grandbaby, and a delayed thanksgiving. Going back to before the celebration, my parents enjoyed last week studying and walking through the markets in Thailand, always on the lookout for that something special for the little one. It's intriguing how being grandparents makes you want to shop constantly, or buy the cutest things you see. Aren't we glad they live in Thailand where stuff is cheap? Back to the present, today was a day we will remember for a very long time, enjoyed by all as we had our family photos taken. Having the fun of three generations present we were able to take some great snap shots, mostly including the new addition to the family. Soon after, we all settled down to a beautiful thanksgiving meal. It was a wonderful time where were all able to share, be thankful and eat some of our favorite foods. Of course on the way home, we realized that the reason we didn't eat my mom's famous sweet potato's was because we had left them in the microwave. But back to that Bible verse I began with. My Dad quoted it to us today as we were talking about what we were truly thankful for. He said, "Personally, I'm thankful for a handbreadth of life: no more, no less. To see three generations here today, I can see God at work, giving us new life, strong mid life, and little by little old and fulfilled life. That would be enough in itself, but to know that it all leads to eternal life in Heaven, that's just something to celebrate!

"Show me, O LORD, my life's end and the number of my days; let me know how fleeting is my life. You have made my days a mere handbreadth; the span of my years is as nothing before you. Each man's life is but a breath. (Psalms 39:4 – 5)

35. A bittersweet time
(February 28th)

We said goodbye on Friday to our kids and boarded the plane to come back to Bangkok. It was a bittersweet time, made more so by the fact that this time, there was one more kid to kiss goodbye. What can I say? Little Isaac Trevor Woods is of course the cutest grandchild ever, and I'm pretty sure that he's already showing signs of giftedness. Nathan and Kylie are the loving and diligent Mum and Dad that we knew they would be, and Nicki is the perfect Auntie.

Tony was reading in the Bible the other day, as you occasionally do when you're a Missionary, and he came across the verse, "My boundary lines have fallen in pleasant places" (Psalms 16:6).

This last week we saw a lot of people with 'boundaries' that are different than ours. There are the restrictive and somewhat daunting boundaries for new parents, not to mention Nicki starting her second year of nursing with all those boundaries of school and assignments. Others were struggling with boundaries of grief, financial trouble, illness and fatigue. We were reminded that each of us enjoy happy, fulfilling days, but then other times we just feel fenced in.

We are back in Bangkok with the ever present boundaries

of pollution, ignorance, poverty and just... the ever present HEAT. I'm sure I'll be feeling a bit trapped this week as we soldier on. It looks like we've got a little more 'push' to go for the finish on the Thai language, and believe me, that's a boundary like a noose. On top of that, our mission is doing some housecleaning and is wondering how we fit in the Bangkok scheme of things as we work primarily with Japanese. Our boundaries as well as our securities may be pushed significantly, but like you, we must remember that the Lord does the placement and his boundaries are pleasant because they're His will.

Wow, it sounds like I should end this blog with something like "May the force be with you"... but then, that's really it, isn't it? May God's force sustain you as you face another week of reality.

LORD, you have assigned me my portion and my cup; you have made my lot secure. The boundary lines have fallen for me in pleasant places; surely I have a delightful inheritance. (Psalms 16:5 -6)

36. True Value
(March 7th)

Today I'd like to give you a little geography lesson. We live in an area of Bangkok that is absolutely full of Japanese businessmen and their families. This is a good thing, because we work mostly with Japanese, and Japanese businessmen are not poor. Our little duplex pre-dates their arrival and sits humbly in amongst all the fancy high rises. To illustrate this point, I must say that I did some hand-to-hand combat with a GIANT cockroach last night. Actually, my hand was on some kind of can with a picture of a lemon on it that shot out yellow goo. I'm not sure who won the battle because after I had trashed the kitchen, I ran upstairs to hide.

Anyway, we have been interested and amused to watch a new little outdoor mall being built at the end of our street. It's called "Japan Town" and now that it's opening up, we find that it sports several upscale coffee shops, Japanese restaurants and the like. Also there is a "True Value" store.

If you're as old as I am and have lived in the USA, you'll remember the joy of going with your dad down to the "True Value" hardware store on a Saturday morning to buy a fan belt, check out the new John Deere tractor or sight in a rifle while catching up with all the "Guy Gossip" in town. Now this "True Value" shop is a real franchise, but even the manager can only refer to his store as a "Too Wall-uu" store because of the inability of the Thai language to accommodate either "R"s, "L"s or most certainly the letter "V".

Within the walls of this small store, we were intrigued to find a nice little array of overpriced Pyrex dishes, pet toys and... a couple of post hole diggers! I'm left wondering WHO would be motivated or even able to dig a hole in the concrete jungle of Bangkok, but...

OK, now let's keep walking perhaps another hundred yards, where if we're agile enough, we can dart thru the traffic and cross a major street. There we enter the largest slum in Bangkok named Klong Toey. When I say "Slum" it's not what we refer to as the wrong side of the tracks... this slum has thousands and thousands of people trapped in gripping poverty, with frequent murders, arson, mafia, drugs, AIDs, you name it. They have little to no access to good education, health or hope, much less post hole diggers.

We love Bangkok more and more each week, where there is almost immediate access to more things than we can imagine, but is that because we live on the 'upside of the street?'

I'll have to say, WHAT is my "True Value"? Is it to plant a lifestyle/culture... even religion that only a privileged few people can access, or is it to show the universal values of the Cross to all God's creatures (with the possible exception of aforementioned cockroach)? I have to ask myself, HOW do I live? Do I really need a post hole digger, or should I cross the street and change one life for the better? Shall I work with Japanese who can possibly change the world with their influence?

Here's a cheap advertisement: We got to see the movie "Blind Side" this week, and it's definitely worth seeing... It's about this very thing. I hope it wins an Oscar.

We'll update you next week on some exciting things that are happening in our ministry. We haven't heard a peep from our mission board about our possible 'relocation' either on paper or... so we'll just put our heads down and keep working, because at the end of the day, who of us knows how much longer we have anyway? ...oh, and we're keeping 'wery wery' quiet.

Have a great week,

Marsha

For where your treasure is, there your heart will be also. (Matthew 6:21)

37. Rising Tensions
(March 14th)

The Thais are a gentle people. If any of you have been watching the news where you are, you will know that the 'red shirts' are converging on Bangkok from all over the country as we speak. These people represent about half the nation, and they want the present administration (the Yellow Shirts) OUT. There are about 10,000 vehicles, all packed to the brims and arriving today. They're hoping for a million or more protestors. Tomorrow they will speak to the government and ask them to dissolve and have (what they consider) a fair election.

Many of you might grow tense when you read about the developing 'situation' here. How many countries have had 'events' like this, with much different and sometimes unfortunate scenarios?

But this is where it becomes *uniquely Thai*. The organizers are asking all the demonstrators to arm themselves with sacks of "Pla Raa"... or what we call 'fermented fish sauce'! You can imagine how this stuff smells and they figure it will act as a GREAT deterrent.

To quote the Bangkok Post, "Mrs Mayuree said that the red shirts need to defend themselves if they are attacked by police or soldiers. Since they will be unarmed, they can repel authorities by throwing bags of pla raa at them.

'We won't rush to throw the bags at them though. It's expensive and it's also our food.'" Mrs. Mayuree said.

We enjoy this country more and more. They have such a sense of fun, and as I mentioned, gentleness. Thank you for continuing to pray for Thailand over the next few days. But try not to say too much in comments or letters back, because seriously, this is a delicate time for us all. And while they are certainly not targeting foreigners at this point, tensions may be running high and we don't want to draw attention to ourselves by speaking out of turn.

We really hope things stay peaceful and they can work out their differences, because if things go wrong, it could get messy... and smelly!

Marsha

Obey your leaders and submit to their authority. They keep watch over you as men who must give an account. Obey them so that their work will be a joy, not a burden, for that would be of no advantage to you.
(Hebrews 13:17)

38. Finding Normal
(March 21st)

Well, today I'm happy to report that it's been a fairly "normal" week around Bangkok.

In spite of being inconvenienced a few times because of the demonstrations, even trapped one day for several hours because all the streets were impassable, it's been a pretty peaceful week. Perhaps because of your prayers. We THINK the whole thing is dying down. The plan changed from throwing the fish sauce and moved toward throwing blood as the week progressed; but apparently it was not well received as the nation's bloodbanks are severely understocked... don't you hate it when a great idea backfires!

I promised I'd tell you about some of the exciting work that is unfolding here for us:

As we mentioned before, the pastor of one of the two Japanese churches has had to return to Japan because of his health. As a result, Tony has stepped in, not to pastor, but to train that church to stand strong and grow forward. It's exciting as there are several really tuned in men and women who Tony will enjoy teaching. He is also carrying most of the preaching load, but that's always a joy for him. He has spent a lot of time this week working with the leaders to introduce a graded Sunday school program which will start soon.

In addition to our continuing language studies, I (Marsha) have started a Bible study for training Christian Japanese women to share their faith. That's going well and is an inspiration to me just teaching such wonderful future leaders. Of course this is usually accompanied by lots of fellowship, lunches, and general goofing off that I'm so good at.

Our Thai language moves forward at pace, hopefully we're almost done... although I still get blindsided frequently, like the other night when the waitress asked me if I wanted "Khaaw suay" (beautiful rice).

"Well" I thought, "DUHH, I don't want UGLY rice! What in the world is she talking about?"

I got my *pretty rice* and the next day the tutor said "that's how we clarify COOKED rice... it's beautiful!" I find it so interesting thinking about how people in other cultures think. We westerners just have "rice", not different delineations, but of course in a RICE CULTURE, you have to specify, and naturally, RAW rice is not going to be that pleasant to eat... or as beautiful!

Lastly, we love Bangkok because it's the crossroads of the world. This weekend we've been visiting with some OLD OLD friends from our days in Zambia. (37 years ago; yikes!!) They're Dutch and we haven't seen them for about 25 years, but as all good friends, we just picked up

where we left off. They're like us in that we just pointed them in the direction of some interesting stuff today and off they went! We weren't free to go with them because of that thing I mentioned, the Japanese ministry!
We hope you have a great week, and please pray for all of our countries!
Marsha (and Tony)

May the favor of the Lord our God rest upon us; establish the work of our hands for us— yes, establish the work of our hands. (Psalms 90:17)

39. Enough?
(March 28th)

We've been thinking about *what's enough* this week. It all started when someone contacted us to say that they had found a 'deal' on a 55 inch state of the art TV. OK, it truly WAS about half price, but as we pondered the issue, we began to think back over the years, and recalled every TV we'd seen in our lives.

Because we are baby boomers, we actually can remember TV about the time it was invented. TV was what other people had and we didn't. TV was what sick rich people had hidden in their cool dark rooms. But then...

When I was about six, we got one, and the world changed. I can still feel the excitement of being all clean from my Saturday night bath, (a weekly event only, can you imagine that now?), hair in curlers, fluttering around the room fighting for position and finally sitting down to watch what I called the "tissue paper dancers" on Lawrence Welk. That, and later the "'Flintstones" were about the only TV our family ever watched.

Then we married and were the proud owners of a 12 inch black and white. Those were the days of that forbidden fruit, "Laugh in," with an occasional "I Love Lucy" or maybe even a "Dragnet" if we felt especially risqué that week.

When we went to Africa, we RENTED a black and white TV just to help stem the boredom of the long dark nights. The TV channel only broadcast for a few hours a night, and I'll never forget the night a cockroach walked across the camera lens on the BROADCASTING side! (It was the live news program). Our fondest memories of that time were laughing to the antics of "Happy Days."

Japan... we were astonished that they didn't even sell black and white anymore. We had to buy a small COLOR TV and felt too guilty to watch it. A few years later we added our first VCR, in the form of a 50 pound camera and battery pack that we justified by saying we'd video the kids, but when they were asleep, we were known to pop in a tape that we'd borrowed from one of our more worldly missionaries.

Then things started progressing more quickly. Bigger TVs, TWO TVs.. finally in 2006 we bought our first flat screen and put it at the foot of our bed...

Now, we're contemplating a 55 INCH state of the art, LED, USB, HD TV. (I think it can even cook and clean!).

Changing the subject (or am I?). On Monday, Tony took our Dutch friends to the slums next door for a cooking class run by World Vision. It included a brief tour of the market where they purchased the ingredients they would be using as well as a visit to the teacher's house.

The house was a two story square the size of your bathroom, perched conveniently over the open sewer. There are EIGHT people living there in relative comfort, as long as they take turns stretching out to sleep. This isn't a problem because they're never home at the same time. Mom and Dad apparently divorced 15 years ago, but had nowhere to go, so they just work around the proximity thing by working different shifts.

I was talking to a girl who is from Burma and is here doing fingernails six days a week. I asked her what she does on Sunday, and she said her "identity card" allows her to go visit her sister in another part of Bangkok. I suggested that she might like to travel, maybe to sightsee or go home to her parents in Burma occasionally, but she said she'd have to have her employer's permission and there wouldn't be time anyway in just one day. I mentioned flying and she said, "Oh no! Once I went to a client's apartment on the 24th floor and I almost got sick, it was so high!"

Life is a gift and a joy, and also a responsibility. We said no to the salesman, because really... 55 inches???

> Then he said to them, "Watch out! Be on your guard against all kinds of greed; a man's life does not consist in the abundance of his possessions." (Luke 12:15)

40. Happy Easter
(April 4th)

This week is the Easter festival all over the world. Unfortunately Thailand hasn't *caught on* to Easter, and it will only be mentioned in the few evangelical churches where there are handfuls of believers. The *junk* associated with Easter isn't even in the stores! This has to be a first, since anything with any commercial possibility was always noted in Japan. Anyway, yesterday the Red Shirts completely froze down the center of the city, forcing all the major shopping areas to close, which you can imagine cost industry a heap of money. Now the Government is getting fed up and are threatening ACTION, so you might want to re kindle our prayers for safety.

Anyway, as this is Easter, I was thinking about what Easter means. All of us who come from a western culture will probably have a lot of memories. I was explaining to some Japanese ladies that until recently Baptists tended to focus on the JOY of the Easter morning. I told them that in my formative years, the most excited I got about Easter was that it meant I had a new dress, and probably a new hat and gloves to match. Definitely new shoes, my new summer ones, because after Easter it was supposed to be summer. And don't forget the Easter

Basket!

Things began to change throughout the years, and Protestants began to realize that Easter came at a price. We started having a thought of a Savior who died on a cross that long ago Friday. Gradually our churches started having Good Friday services for reflection and thanksgiving, stopping to think about what Christ had done. We began to realize that this was hard for Jesus. He wasn't looking forward to it. But He did it because He loves us.

Last Sunday I took a friend to visit the big church our mission supports for paroled prisoners. Tony no longer is able to go around with me to visit Thai churches, because he's preaching at least every Sunday, and that's his life and he loves it, but since we're technically still in language study, I'm still roaming around looking for good services in Thai when I'm not involved in Japanese as well. Anyway my goal for the morning was to deliver some hotel amenities that the ladies in Australia had collected. When prisoners are released, they have literally NOTHING and the "House of Blessing" church ministers to them in their new life. As you can imagine, a small bottle of shampoo or hand lotion is really appreciated. I always enjoy going to this church because the services are full of passion and excitement, ex-prisoners and their families celebrating the joy of new lives in Christ. It's exciting to worship there. I especially like it that the preacher is preaching to the illiterate and unchurched, so he keeps the sermons simple. Often I can understand a bit of the Thai, which gives validation to this ongoing study of ours. And I can certainly understand the feeling!

The music is amazing. All members of the worship team have served time, and probably the only music they ever came in contact with was the electric drone of the red light districts. This *upbeat tempo* communicates well into Gospel songs and as they lift the volume to the max, you can't help but join in.

As I was belting out the choruses, there came the surprise. The key changed, the music slowed a little, but the volume was confident and I realized they were singing a familiar but almost forgotten tune. "To God Be the Glory!" What a surprise! My friend and I glanced at each other in astonishment and sang along at the top of our lungs because well... that was my Daddy's favorite song. I can remember so many times, especially Sunday nights, when old deacon Bob Smith would request that song, and I'd sing at the top of my lungs then too, because I was so proud of my godly father.

Now I was singing it in Thai, (at least my version of Thai) with a hundred or more ex-cons, saved or being saved by grace... My friend and I both had tears running down our faces when the song finally finished.

This week as you read the news and wonder what's going on, and where the world is headed, we have to remember that the Gospel is spread right round the world, to sinners saved by a Man on a cross.

"To God Be the Glory... Great things he hath done!!!"

God bless you,

Marsha

Be exalted, O God, above the heavens; let your glory be over all the earth. (Psalms 57:11)

41. Sad Times in Thailand
(April 11th)

Sad times in Thailand.

Well, I no sooner got this week's blog up than the news came in about the tragic turn of events in Bangkok yesterday. Without getting involved in the politics of the situation, all we can say is that the situation seems to have escalated and at last count 21 lives have been lost. It breaks out heart to see this, because we honestly believe that neither side wanted this to happen. But with so many people in such close proximity the chance of things getting out of hand grows daily. Please pray with us for a quick resolution and no more loss of life.

As it turns out, Tony and I didn't hear the news until today (Sunday) because we're up in the northern city of Chiangmai at the invitation of the Japanese church here. We'll be coming back in May and June to fill the pulpit and lead lots of Bible studies and training sessions while the pastor is in Japan. It's really exciting to have a chance to help raise up dedicated Japanese Christians for the task of bringing the Gospel to lots more than we'll ever reach, and to do it better than we ever could. The Japanese church back in Bangkok has grudgingly given their approval for our being away for several weeks because, first, they have no choice, and second, they really are keen to see if they can actually keep things going without both pastor AND "pastor advisor". We think they can, and this time of forced independence will be a great litmus test both for them as well as for us. Are we teaching the right things the right way? Are they taking it on board? We'll all know soon! Thanks for your prayers.

Meantime, the country is going into the biggest week of the year, Sonkhran, which is their New Year's and also that time when it's absolutely permissible to pour, bucket, squirt, and douse water all over whoever you can. The result is a week-long water fight. EVERYONE participates, and it's welcome in the searing heat. Today, just driving back from church, our car got pelted every few yards, mostly by kids armed with 55 gallon drums of water for instant refills of their plastic buckets. We were quite grateful that we were able to keep the windows rolled up, even as we pitied the poor souls on motorbikes!

Again, thanks for your prayers for Thailand, and for all those who have found themselves in a difficult and sometimes dangerous situation. Pray that this will be a time of discovery, as God's love and mercy pours out like that Sonkhran water.

Marsha

As the deer pants for streams of water, so my soul pants for you, O God. My soul thirsts for God, for the living God. When can I go and meet with God?
(Psalms 42:1 – 2)

42. A Roller Coaster Week
(April 18th)

I was hanging out the laundry one night this last week... you may think that's strange, but it's HOT here in Bangkok, and somehow wet clothes at night seem a little more pleasant. As I reached up to attach a shirt to the clothes line, my eye caught something glittering higher up. I had to stop and think for a minute and then I realized it was one brave little STAR! In a city of 13 million, I could see a STAR!

Maybe this phenomena happened because this last week was the Thai New Year called Songkhran. For three days, no one comes to work, all the polluters, (factories, etc) are closed and most people try to get home to the family, leaving the city fairly deserted. Many of you have heard of the famous water fights associated with Songkhran, and we got to participate. What a riot! All of us "farangs" as they call foreigners, have decided that this is the perfect answer to a lot of things. It's terribly hot, so what better 'relief' than to take to the streets to douse, squirt and smear paste made of talcum powder and water on everything and everybody you see. From ancient times it's been considered a 'blessing', but it's also just good wholesome fun! We saw literally thousands and thousands of the most well behaved youth, just laughing and gently tossing water on each other. Of course there was the occasional mischievous one with a water hose, but it was really tame. We happened into the middle of them; some of them even excused themselves with a polite "Khatort Khap" before they totally smeared our faces.

Of course the other 'event' that's carried on all week was the continuing struggle with the Red Shirts. The dramas have been large, but as far as we know there have been no more killings, and the 'fight' seems to be mostly confined to places that you just know to avoid. It's not over yet. Apparently, one of the primary leaders slipped away from arrest by being let down from the third floor in the back of the hotel where he was staying. The police chief that let him get away has now been replaced by a military officer. Who can predict if he'll do any better at catching the perpetrators. Stores and offices remained closed with the occasional interruption of trains and busses and 'living' is inconvenient, but everyone is taking it in their stride. I'll be curious if tempers flare this next week when everyone has to resume business.

Oh, and then there's the volcano!... Thousands and thousands of European, English and every other imaginable traveler have been stranded here. Our friend who is a pilot is stranded in Singapore and he writes that he doesn't know WHEN he'll ever receive orders even to go home!

We live in uncertain times. You might see an unexpected wonder of nature or have some fun with water... or find yourself wondering how in the 21st century people can just disappear! What I do know is this: Life is never boring in the service of the Lord, don't you think? [Note: In the original blog, included here was the story of the mysterious disappearance of the parents of a Vietnamese couple, whose children were faithful members of a local church. It was later learned that they had been snatched by unidentified agents and smuggled back to Vietnam, where they were accused of "terrorism". The children were eventually taken under the wing of the United Nations and moved to another country and safety. But for several weeks, the situation was tense, as the agents attempted to abduct the children as well. Tony and Marsha were caught up in the drama, passing along money and support in secret. It soon became apparent that they were also "persons of interest" by the agents, and so they removed all evidence of their knowledge from the web site].

Thanks for your prayers,

Marsha

"For I am convinced that neither death nor life, neither angels nor demons, neither the present nor the future, nor any powers, neither height nor depth, nor anything else in all creation, will be able to separate us from the love of God that is in Christ Jesus our Lord."
(Romans 8:38-39)

43. I've decided I Like Movies
(April 25th)

I've decided I like movies...

In the movies, you almost immediately can figure out WHO the bad guys are and can relax, only occasionally shouting out comments like "Don't go with him, you'll be sorry" or "Duhh... can't you SEE what she's up to?" the like.

Life has not been a very good movie this last week. We have the "Bad Guys" who snatched the parents (see last week's blog), but we're not able to figure out the plot. The parents have been found, back in their former country's prison and whereas there's some relief to know they're alive, they're definitely not better off. Apparently like the Old Testament, the aforementioned bad guys are aiming for revenge 'to the next generation', sending messages of such thru Mom's confiscated cell phone and putting us all in a panic as to how to help/hide/save the six innocent offspring. Some progress is being made (think of the big multinational guys with the pretty building in NYC) but it's still a real cliff hanger. Please continue to pray HARD!

The other drama (you know how movies have several plots going at the same time?) is the escalating struggle with the Reds vs Yellows. This one is a case of "WHO in the world IS the bad guy?" There IS a pretty good explanation on CNN news online if you're interested, but this week the "Multi Colors" (a newly formed group that's saying, "would Y'all just STOP fighting"?) entered in... there were some grenades launched and three people are dead and something like 88 injured as a result. Nobody knows "who" launched the grenades, but they landed right where we were having our hilarious water fight just two weeks ago (this is where the audience says a corporate 'ohhhh!'). The challenge and 'fun' of this big adventure is beginning to wear at us. A couple of nights ago we could hear gunfire right here in our quiet little neighborhood. That's getting creepy. The train thru the city is closed in several places and it stops running at 6PM, further inconveniencing everyone in town.

Now if we can just get on to the grand (happy) ending, we'll breathe a sigh of relief and get on with our lives. Thailand is such a beautiful, peaceful place, surrounded with countries who have had political disaster; we just want it to be back to where it was. Our mission, we are confident, will tell us when it's time to run. The American embassy apparently is sending out emails to those who are registered. (Oops, we have forgotten to do this but will soon!) These emails are saying, "Stay out of Bangkok". Tony's just told me that the military now has full authority to 'move on the Reds' and reclaim downtown, but will not announce when they plan to do this. I'm guessing it will be soon.

Meanwhile, we're eating, sleeping, talking to the kids on Skype and the rest of you on Facebook. Tony's preparing to preach to the handful of Japanese who will brave going out doors... after all, besides the demonstrations, it's HOT, you know! I will teach my last Bible study on Monday before we go OUT OF TOWN (yeah!) next week for our first annual Thai Baptist Convention. I'm sure I'll have the 'Massive Headache of not understanding the language' the whole week, but it's at the Baptist camp and should be interesting anyway. It'll be nice to meet the Thais that are so faithful in the face of such opposition.

God is still Good, and we are still doing fine. In three weeks we move to Chiang Mai for six weeks of INTENSE work in a small Japanese church. We may be tired, but hopefully be able to relax with less inconvenience because of political problems.

ONE very happy ending...... we just found out that we made the grade with the Thai language and can move on into full time ministry! We are ELATED and feel like we've been given a gift of our lives back, since we've been doing full time ministry, as well as trying to get in the Thai study for the last several months anyway.

Live the life of a believer! And we'll see you next week!

All my longings lie open before you, O Lord; my sighing is not hidden from you. (Psalms 38:9)

44. Out to Lunch
(May 2nd)

The blog will be down for a little while. If you're on our mailing list, watch for updates. Thanks,
Marsha

Keep me as the apple of your eye; hide me in the shadow of your wings from the wicked who assail me, from my mortal enemies who surround me.
(Psalms 17:8 – 9)

[Note: It was at this point that Tony and Marsha decided to go "off the grid" entirely until they could assess the threat level of the still unidentified agents who had snatched the parents and were actively pursuing the six children throughout Bangkok. By the following week, it was determined that while it was already too late to hide their involvement, the best plan would be to assure anyone watching that Tony and Marsha had no useful information. Thus, next week's blog].

45. A Clean Slate
(May 16th)

I think I'm flattered. A few weeks ago, I mentioned that if you wanted to know more about this kidnap drama we've been chronicling, you could google this certain name and see what the yellow journalism was saying... well, to my surprise, several hours later, a friend messaged us to say that OUR blog was in the number two place on the list of 8 pages. That means (I think) that our blog had received a deluge of hits, almost putting it in the number one slot of interest. That should be a good thing, but since our blog was mostly regaling our opinions about the eight other pages, using words like "trumped up charges" and "draconian tactics", I read it with a great deal of concern, not sure if I wanted to be brought to the attention of the people I was slandering. I'm beginning to understand that these guys really know how to hold a grudge and are actively looking to kill anyone they think is an accessory. (I can fill you in with more facts off line). Unfortunately, after several unsuccessful evasive techniques, (Google is hard to crack into) we had to just drop off the internet and lay low for a few weeks. Now, I think we're finally gone from the site and hopefully from the interest of the bad guys. Let's call it a lesson learned that, as my mother used to say to my dad when they needed to talk privately, "there are too many ears in the cornfield here". The internet may be our friend, but our foes can access it just as easily.

Let me say now, that the afore mentioned situation is still a worry, and it's definitely not over, but the G*d of the universe is in control and while we know NO DETAILS, (honestly), the children, we believe are temporarily safe. Barring a miracle, we believe the parents are probably gone, but if you've read "Heavenly Man" you know miracles can and do happen. Stay tuned and pr*y for a world that hasn't changed much in centuries.

And of course the other 'drama' is Bangkok. The American Embassy said last night that they were allowing their families of personnel to leave. That's never a good sign. Our mission office is just two blocks from the worst of the fighting, but consider themselves safe for the time being. They did decide to cancel worship services today, as did every other church close to the barricades, but home groups will continue. Our little intrepid Japanese group decided to go ahead with worship, even though many will not be able to get to church, and besides their "pastor advisor" (Tony) is off to the boondocks for six weeks! It's very sad and Thailand is getting more and more confused as to how to get out of this whole thing gracefully. We love Thailand and pray that they'll be able to work this out and get back to being a beacon amidst some rather difficult countries.

We are happy that the timing for us to be gone has so seamlessly worked out and we have 'escaped' to a safer kinder place up north, hopefully free of both Red Shirts and the VC! We were asked several months ago to assist a Japanese church here while the pastor, after eight years, takes a break back to Japan. We chose to ride the train and the normal 14 hour trip took over 18, five hours without air conditioning. It was fun, especially since we'd gone through two different people who were supposed to pick us up and were finally left with a disgusted "just go out the front and the white SUV will have the keys under the mat!" Tony loves this cloak and dagger stuff. We'll be here for five Sundays, and are very excited. We'll probably work harder than we have in Bangkok, which is hard to believe, since Bangkok was busy, but anyway, it'll be challenging! This morning we had a wonderful time meeting the congregation. They were so enthusiastic and are a truly remarkable bunch... one guy, from the Kachin race of people from Burma, speaks seven languages and met Christ and his wife in Japan... we look forward to getting to know them better in the next few weeks.

Another challenge will be living in one room. I told Tony, "We're really getting ready for the nursing home!" A church member has graciously lent us her apartment. It is one room, a toilet with a shower head stuck on a bare wall, and a balcony to lean over. It's over 100 degrees outside here, so the air conditioner is definitely the 'charm point' of the room. Another 'charm point' is that she also has given us the use of an identical room across the hall! We decided that we'd miss each other if he lived over there, and the A/C bill would be too much, so we're using that as the 'wet' shower room, and storage for all the churchy paraphernalia that we brought to train and run a church. Of course, if you decide to visit, we'll clear off the bed!

Thanks for your pr*yers, I hope your week is peaceful and safe as we trust ours to be.

Marsha and Tony

The angel of the LORD encamps around those who fear him, and he delivers them. (Psalms 34:7)

46. You Are
(May 24th)

We were buying food, vaguely aware that we needed to 'stock up' in case things got worse. Suddenly there was a loud announcement and thankfully we could understand enough Thai to realize they were saying we had ten minutes to exit the store. What we didn't realize was that in light of the events in Bangkok, there was now a 7PM curfew on all the country. As we drove home, we could see the smoke from fires burning throughout the city. Not Bangkok, but the city in the far north where we thought we were safe. This has been a week to remember. As a white western civilization citizen I'm not used to being truly frightened, but this week gave me a taste of what it's like to literally not know what will happen next to the place you call home or the people you love. Although we had, as we mentioned last week, safely moved to the town in the far north, we watched with horror as Bangkok burned. We thought of people we knew and tried to reach them, sometimes succeeding sometimes not. We wondered what we had of value that needed to be rescued if the word came to evacuate, and even though we didn't need to physically evacuate ourselves, what about our possessions? Remember when I wrote the blog about "Enough?" Again, I had to ponder what really I needed to have someone go into my house and rescue... or not. In the end, it wasn't necessary to physically evacuate more than our bodies, and most of our personnel that fled for the countryside are now beginning to trickle back. I've heard of no damage to any of our personal property although the fires and shooting did come fairly near our house. The young couple who live next door were virtually trapped by the fighting, but started their missionary career by being brave and keeping their heads down. I wish I could be more poetic, perhaps attaching a pithy meaning to all of this, but I'm still too stunned. In the words of one of the latest songwriters, You are God of this city, You are King of this nation, You are hope for the hopeless, You Are. Please Pray for Thailand. Marsha and Tony

O LORD, I say to you, "You are my God." Hear, O LORD, my cry for mercy. O Sovereign LORD, my strong deliverer, who shields my head in the day of battle— (Psalms 140:6 – 7)

47. Elephants and Such
(May 30th)

It's been a much better week. The prime minister has announced that "after ten days, Thailand has been restored to peace", so we can all breathe a sigh of relief. The curfews are gone, Bangkok, as we understand, is pretty well cleaned up and hopefully the burned out buildings will be rebuilt in six months or so. Apparently there was a huge effort by the citizens to pitch in and help with the cleanup... Thai people are so lovely.

This week we got an interesting letter from one of our church members in Bangkok. It was just the general housekeeping stuff that you would write a pastor who is out of town for six weeks. What caught my eye was his closing, in rather quaint English.

"Please I hope Lord Defend you..." I suppose he meant to say "protect" but as I thought about the difference in words, I thought about 'defend'. Does the Lord 'defend' as well as protect me?

Now let's think about something else. This last Friday we were able to sneak away to a little hamlet in the mountains here called "Pai". Apparently it was 'discovered' to be a sleepy little village by a bunch of tuned in dropped out hippies in the 60's and the rest is history. The town looks like the tourist town you're bound to have in your area.

You can buy every imagination of T-shirt proclaiming that you've survived the 752 hairpin curves getting there or you've found the "Pai in the sky". I've heard the night life is not to be missed.

We, on the other hand, chose a quiet little guest house on the outskirts of town that sports a hot spring. You know us, once a Japanese bath fan, always a Japanese bath fan. So there we were, happily lazing away in the water, when what should appear but two ELEPHANTS and their requisite Mahouts. They came up to eat the grass and give their keepers a rest in the shade. Before we knew it, the Mahouts shouted to us to come over and see them.

Armed with our wealth of Thai, (this is a joke) and with me trying to keep my swimsuit cover up from falling off, we were able to go over and have a chat. We ascertained that the elephants, named "Ott" and something I couldn't pronounce, were 20 and 29 yrs old. We laughed together that those are exactly the ages of our children. One of the Mahout's name was LuLu and I was able to suppress a laugh, while punching Tony who thought that was the Elephant's name (as it probably should have been).

Then they said, "Let's go over and visit with them!"

Gingerly, we advanced. Do you have any idea how BIG a young adult Elephant IS? This was the first time

I'd approached such a beast without at least a stick of bamboo between us.

Now let's go back to the 'defend' idea. Do you remember in the book Narnia, Lucy is talking about the lion (who represents Christ) and she says "is he safe?" The beavers answer, "Safe? Of course not, he's a Lion (God) but he IS the king."

That's the way I felt. Was the Elephant SAFE? No! LuLu could perhaps protect me, but could he DEFEND me? No. Just this week there have been reports of several people in India killed by 'rogue' elephants. Standing there, I realized that if "Ott" didn't like the looks of me or the color of my sagging sarong, and decided to reach forward and fling me to kingdom come, there was nothing that LuLu could do to DEFEND me. It was indeed a frightening thought.

Paul said in Romans 5:8, "In that while we were yet sinners, Christ died for us." Isn't it just awesome that He not only protects us but DEFENDS us, with his blood, against a fate truly 'worse than death?'

On a final note... our little family that's in hiding... many of you know about this and are praying. Apparently the large multinational organization that is working with them is now moving from the status of "protector" to the bureaucratic "we are the biggest and the best and we know everything so you must obey us while we drag

our feet" aggressive status. Those six precious children need our DEFENDING prayers badly. Please PRAY! Again, let me remind you that we've discovered that this is not a 'safe' world, so please don't do or say anything on the internet about this situation, just talk to the One who can actually Defend. Please pray that the enemy's eyes would be blinded as they continue to search for them to destroy them. Pray for Godspeed and patience with all involved and lastly pray for courage for the kids. We'll keep you posted as we hear.
Marsha

A father to the fatherless, a defender of widows, is God in his holy dwelling. (Psalms 68:5)

48. Keeping the Pace
(June 6th)

Three miles is a long way to walk in high humidity and heat, all the while remembering Thai modesty by refraining from sleevelessness or shorts. We set out this week (for the second time) to 'walk the moat' around the old city section of Chiang Mai.

Each side is just over a kilometer long, and by the fourth side, the temperature had soared, we hadn't had anything to drink, and we were beginning to feel that we needed to pick up the pace and get back to work. I began to experience what I've heard others call "punch drunk". You could have knocked me over with a feather, which is not a good position in Thailand. And keep in mind that it's impossible to walk either straight or steadily. There are just too many people, broken sidewalks, bare electric cables, vendors, cars, trucks, motorcycles... not to mention the ubiquitous 'store attached to a motorcycle' that will be zipping along hoping to find a customer for his sausages or brooms or whatever and... you get the picture.

Being punch drunk is a bad way to be. Tony was far ahead of me, off in his own world imagining he was a Burmese warrior storming the city, this time for GOD! ...anyway, way too focused on the goal to turn around and see if I was still alive. Sweat was literally streaming into my eyes restricting my vision as well. Flies began to pester me, my own mind betrayed me and, instead of bolstering me up with happy thoughts of cool breezes and the like, berated me with "what kind of a wimp are you, this is not a mountain. Why are you so wiped out?" I had to wonder whose idea this adventure had been anyway... and more importantly, WHAT WAS THE POINT?

We've been in the little Japanese church here in Chiang Mai for five weeks. We've had a ball; it's been refreshing to have such enthusiastic people who are so desperate to study the Bible and be trained for service.

But it's been a little bit like walking the moat. It just seems to never let up! We come home exhausted without an ounce of energy left, all from fielding DEEP spiritual questions, teaching new thinking, healing hurts, defending the Bible... of course all in Japanese, which causes Tony and I to have to work harder just to discern what they are saying and think of ways to respond in such a way that they can understand.

We're exhausted, but it's a good kind of tired. Once we missionaries were likened to 'marathon runners' as opposed to the volunteer teams that came over for a couple of weeks at a time and were labeled, "sprinters." We look at the long haul and pace ourselves. I guess because of the nature of this particular assignment; to get this one church up and running strong, we've been 'sprinting' and now we're almost to the finish line... at least for Chiang Mai. We won't forget this race and the people that made it so much fun!

But don't get me wrong, we're not congratulating ourselves or wanting you to think we've done something really hard. We're just stating that sometimes the work is hard... but rewarding. Like Paul, we think it's worth doing, even if during the push you might stop and think, "Will I make it?" or "Who's idea was this anyway?"

Run the race... at the pace and place God tells you.

Marsha

PS. One more note on that other 'race' we've been mentioning in guarded words... I remember when we adopted Nicki and had hit the wall with the Embassy, thinking, "Who can you go to that's higher than the Embassy?" In this case we might add the UN as well, as both they and the embassies are dragging their feet while (it seems to me) playing tough with the frightened ones. "Do as we say or else" kind of stuff. I do know that they are all in two rooms (everyone I know is against them being together but powers that be insist.) They are relatively safe because they don't go out, but their nerves are fraying. Please, please pray for something to break thru soon!! Oh, and the "higher than the Embassy" is duhhhhh... you guessed it, the GOD of the UNIVERSE, the HELPER of the HELPLESS. PRAY HARD!!!

Fourteen years later I went up again to Jerusalem, this time with Barnabas. I took Titus along also. I went in response to a revelation and set before them the gospel that I preach among the Gentiles. But I did this privately to those who seemed to be leaders, for fear that I was running or had run my race in vain.
(Galatians 2:1 – 2)

49. Cycles
(June 13th)

When you read this I will have just finished my fith cycle. Sounds sort of medical, but let me explain to all of you readers with round eyes.

In the Chinese calendar, which dominates Asian superstition, there are 12 animals, each one representing a year. This year is the "year of the Tiger". I'm a Tiger. Coincidentally our first Grandson is also a tiger. I give absolutely NO CREDENCE to these things, but I do think it's interesting that some of the qualities match my personality. Such things as 'loving a challenge' and being 'brave'... I choose to ignore the faults such as 'loves attention' and the like.

So if you can do the math, you've reasoned that 12×5 makes me 60 today. My next 'cycle' of 12 years will (hopefully) land me at 72, etc. I'm happy to say that I feel like 30, but the mirror unfortunately tells me differently. I read somewhere that '60 is the youth of old age' but I also find myself more and more taking the Ronald Reagan approach who said, "You know you're getting old when you pick the alternative that'll get you home at 9:00".

Today we wrapped up five weeks of work in Chiang Mai. It's been a joy! I can't remember a more enjoyable work assignment. The service today had several first time visitors, including one older man who'd never been in a church but had read (somehow) Tony's book and came with tears in his eyes, saying, "I related to what you said about 'wrestling with God' and now your sermon has answered the rest of my questions." Tony was able to pray with him and I hope you'll continue to pray that he finds the family he's looking for in Christ. What a great day!

We are flying out tonight to the island of Phuket, in southern Thailand, where Tony has vowed to do his best to welcome me into the 60's. I hope he can do it in the few days of relaxation that we're taking... and doesn't involve shuffleboard! Then it's back to Bangkok and the people waiting there. We're excited.

My birth mother died when I was 14. When I think of what a bewildered little girl I was then, I have to say in retrospect that God has been VERY VERY good to me. I think of another 14 year old here in Thailand who weighs 18 Kilos (39 lbs) and is losing a battle with AIDS. Our other around-14-yr-old refugee kids that we talk about every week have truly lost their Mother... along with their Father... and have no idea if they'll ever see them again. These girls aren't 'tigers' but they are trusting God every day... and they are VERY brave.

As I think about my blessed life, my wonderful husband

and kids and my mission that's always 'interesting' to work for, I'll never forget a song my mother picked for her funeral, most of you (if you're as old as I am) know it, I think it's called 'Satisfied'. I just remember these words, "But the question comes to me as I think of Calvary, is my Master satisfied with me?" ...haunting stuff. I hope He is, I'm certainly satisfied with Him.

We've had some other rather 'interesting news' this week, but I'm sure you can wait till next week, eh?? After all, I'm old now and it'll probably take me longer to get the blog together.

Marsha

"Be strong and courageous. Do not be afraid or terrified because of them, for the LORD your God goes with you; he will never leave you nor forsake you."
(Deuteronomy 31:6)

50. Harvest Time
(June 20th)

After last week's awesome testimony from the man who found his way to church after reading Tony's book, we've been basking in the after glow of a fruitful time in Chiang Mai. Who would have thought the harvest was just beginning!

This morning after the worship service, Esaka san stood up to quietly blow us all away. Before going to Chiang Mai, he and Tony had prayed together. He was honestly seeking Christ, but a number of things, including the fact that his Thai wife was not a Christian, were holding him back. Tony prayed that sometime soon, God would show him something absolutely amazing... something which would throw all of his doubts aside and bring him to belief. This morning, Esaka san shared with the church that he and his wife had actually been in counseling, and for some unknown reason they both decided to attend a local Thai church (first time for both of them). She heard the Gospel in her own language, it took, and she became a Christian! This may mean that we lose him to another church, but the whole family coming to Christ is worth it!

Then God spoke to Tony and me from the mouth of another seeker. I'm still not sure what prompted his testimony, but it was just what we needed to hear. It was a well-known story supposedly from Confucius.

It seems that a man came to the wall of a great city. He was carrying all his personal belongings and called out to the gatekeeper, "I'm moving to this city, what sort of place is it?" The gatekeeper shouted back, "What sort of city did you leave?" "Horrible," he answered. "Full of tricksters, bad food and people who were always fighting and cheating me. I never want to go back to that city for sure!" The Gatekeeper replied, "I'm sorry to tell you, but I'm afraid you'll find the same thing here. It's a terrible place." The next day another stranger approached the gate. "Hey Gatekeeper!" he called out, "What sort of city is this? I'm moving here!" The gatekeeper answered in the same way, "What sort of place did you leave?" "Oh! It was a beautiful city, full of loving and accepting people, I was so happy there and I'm hoping I'll find the same thing here!" The Gatekeeper said, "Welcome home, we've been waiting for you!"

I promised you some big news last week in the blog, but I'm afraid we're going to take another week to get our minds and our luggage together. We'll let you know as soon as we can. Meanwhile, we're thinking about what kinds of cities we've lived in. What about you?

Love,

Marsha

Let us not become weary in doing good, for at the proper time we will reap a harvest if we do not give up.
(Galatians 6:9)

51. Changes
(June 27th)

We were walking down our street to the train station yesterday. I heard something loud and somehow 'different' and turned just in time to see a man flying thru the air at about head level. He hit the pavement and tumbled two or three times, coming to a stop about ten feet behind his still moving motorcycle. His helmet, which I assume was just perched on his head as is the fashion, landed further down the street like a football bouncing thru the goal posts.

Tony, ever the ambulance driver, rushed to the man, who was just lying there. I stepped out into the street to stop the traffic with my ever widening girth. The man stirred and tried to get up, and after Tony had given him a cursory check, helped him to his feet. Obviously stunned but otherwise in one piece, we believe that he wasn't injured too bad. His motorbike however, did not fare as well, meaning that he'd lost it and therefore his livelihood, as he is a motorcycle taxi man. When everything was relocated to the side of the road, we exchanged bows with the bystanders and continued on, a little shaken, but glad it was no worse.

How our lives can change in the blink of an eye. I have no idea what caused the accident. I hope it wasn't the sight of us walking along that distracted him, but I think not, since this is Bangkok and 'farang' or foreigners, aren't that unusual... however something caused him to lose control.

Our dear dear friend and co-worker for 30+ years, Kumiko Ito, breathed in at the wrong moment sometime last year, and her cells began to grow in that mutant way called Cancer, and in what seems to be the blink of an eye, has either already gone to be with the Lord or will be going soon. We are flying to Japan as this letter goes out to be with the family. She was so young, with her first grandbaby on the way... we have a thousand questions as to why such a hard worker for the Gospel would be called home so early. We will miss her greatly. Please pray that we can be of some help to the family as we are there for a few days before returning to our busy schedules here.

And now, the news I've been putting off telling you:

You may remember a few months ago I quoted the verse in Psalms 16:6 that says "my boundaries have fallen in pleasant places?" Well, in the blink of an eye, we have had our boundary lines moved rather abruptly! In a sweet but succinct letter, our mission has recalled us to Japan!

We are shocked, and have spent a fair bit of time wailing and banging our heads on the wall, but at the same time flattered that they are telling us we really are needed. They say that they understand our work in Thailand is significant, but, because of the terrible lostness of Japan, as well as the mission force being down by about 90% from the time we left, they feel that we're needed far more in Japan. We wonder how it is that we could be used more effectively, but are trusting God to show us.

As we have processed this decision, we feel more and more that two things are going to happen: (1) God will take care of the Thailand based Japanese. We've seen more and more verification of this as we work and train with them here. They are really a great bunch of people and we have utmost confidence in them. (2) God will not fail to show us something amazing about going back to Japan. Even now as we think about life without our friend Kumiko, we wonder what her passing will bring to the ongoing witness of God to the Japanese.

Pray with us. We have been graciously given till the end of the year (six months) to enjoy our Thai brothers and sisters (and newly learned language) and to lay on the training and evangelism with fervor before moving back to Japan in January. ONLY because we trust God are we happy about this. He has never failed us. The mission's been pretty good to us over the years as well, so we're trusting them as well.

If any of you would like the 'longer letter', please don't

hesitate to ask and we'll send it to you.
God is good. Marsha

Oh! This just in! Our little refugees will be sent to... SWEDEN! Again, lots of questions, but as Oswald Chambers said this morning, "Don't enthrone common sense and then hang God's Name on it!" The kids, having never been cold a day in their lives or certainly never having seen snow are in for a treat!

Let the morning bring me word of your unfailing love, for I have put my trust in you. Show me the way I should go, for to you I lift up my soul.
(Psalms 143:8)

52. Saying Goodbye
(July 4th)

This week we said goodbye to one of our dearest friends in Japan. We have known Kumiko and her husband Shinkichi, for over 30 years, and have worked side by side, laughed, cried, raised each other's kids and participated in their weddings. These are the friends you call up when you decide to roast hotdogs in your fireplace. More importantly, these are the friends who'll point out when you're wrong but rejoice with you when you succeed.

Kumiko has to be one of the most physically fit and beautiful (both inside and out) women I've ever known. Yet, even though she had boundless energy and never shirked a challenge, she just couldn't beat the cancer that took her life about this time last Sunday.

We were trying to get there in time, but had to be content to just thank her, as her children held the phone to her ear, and remind her that we'd see her in heaven. When the pastor there reminded those in the room that she'd be seeing our son soon, she smiled. A few minutes later she said, "Jesus is here!" then she added, "Shepherds! The shepherds have come!" and she passed peacefully into heaven.

We arrived a few hours later, and jumped into the several

days of celebration and goodbyes that are involved in a Japanese funeral. Kumiko's body was resting in a simple coffin right there in the small room with us all together, and as we talked, laughed, and ate, we could feel her presence with us. Then after the second large church service of hundreds of people on the third day, we proceeded (rather poetically in the pouring rain), up the lonely hill to the crematorium.

When our son Trevor was cremated, it was just a matter of filling out the paperwork and then having his body picked up at the hospital in a sealed urn a few days later. Not so in Japan. When we arrived at the crematorium, the coffin was carried into a small room, and once again we sang, prayed, and said goodbye. One by one the family and close friends put flowers in around her body, had one last individual minute with her, and then the family shut down the lid. From the back of the crowd someone started singing, quietly at first, and then with conviction, a beautiful old hymn, and we proceeded, pushing the coffin, to the oven, knowing we'd never again see her in this world.

The doors closed, and we were ushered into yet another room to wait. It was a bittersweet time while everyone talked and ate and remembered things about her, how much better her cooking was than what we were eating now, or how hard she'd worked for the Lord, what a beautiful young bride she was, how she'd loved us all. Someone else mentioned how she had learned to drive just so she could be at church during the week, and how the first time she drove out in the early evening, she was driving so carefully, her son had said, "Look Mommy, there's a PARADE behind us!" ...and we'd laugh again, wiping tears and missing her already.

After a couple of hours, Shinkichi (her husband) came over and said, "Come with me, her bones are beautiful". We got up and walked back to the room, and there, on a tray, was all that was left of Kumiko on this earth. Just a part of a skull and a few very white and fragmented, but 'beautiful' white bones. Using chopsticks, each of us picked up a bone to be placed in the urn.

I picked a rib, because it was near her heart, where I hope I will always remain.

One of her favorite verses was Philippians 3:10, where Paul says with Kumiko, "I want to KNOW Christ and the power of his resurrection and the fellowship of sharing in his sufferings, becoming like Him in His death."

Thank you Kumiko for making our lives so rich.

Marsha

If we have been united with him like this in his death, we will certainly also be united with him in his resurrection. (Romans 6:5)

53. Short But Sweet!
(July 11th)

Friends, this week has been a busy one, but pretty (thankfully) mundane. Right now we're in Chiang Mai again at our annual meetings, so it's pretty full on. I would very much like you to PRAY for safety for our little ones... the six that we've been keeping you updated on [Note: the Vietnamese kids whose parents were snatched and smuggled back to Vietnam]. This next Wednesday night here, which is Wednesday morning in the US, they have to make one last VERY DANGEROUS trip... to the airport. Because of the corrupt police, I'm trusting God that nobody bribes the authorities, and they arrive safe and sound to begin their journey of a lifetime. NEXT WEEK we hope to tell you all the good news. Love you all, thanks for keeping us in your prayers.

Even though I walk through the valley of the shadow of death, I will fear no evil, for you are with me; your rod and your staff, they comfort me. (Psalms 23:4)

54. Good News
(July 18th)

Today we got the news we've been waiting for.
The six children we've mentioned before have been waiting for eight and a half YEARS to be free. A few months ago I wrote a blog outlining the horror of their parents being kidnapped and taken back to the nearby country to be put in prison and at best only tortured (But we fear the worst). Immediately I attracted the attention of all the associated bad guys who were looking for the kids, and we spent an anxious few weeks looking over OUR shoulders. The internet is a scary thing, and that's why I'm talking rather vaguely even now.
ANYWAY, last Wednesday night, thanks to your prayers, the children all arrived safely at the airport. Four of them had been subjected to a terrifying week in JAIL because they had come into Thailand without permission eight years ago when they were fleeing for their lives! After a tearful reunion with each other and good byes to those who have supported them this long time, they lifted off on the first plane ride of their lives. About 24 hours later, after three layovers and a long bus ride, they arrived at their new home, deep in a forest somewhere not far from the north pole. There they found six pillows, six blankets and six towels all lined up waiting for them. They said

that they just couldn't believe they were so 'warmly' welcomed. They're in a two bedroom flat and are at a loss as to how to spread out that much, having never had more than one room for the whole family. Yesterday, we heard that it was 18 degrees Celsius and raining, so they're freezing, but deliriously happy.

Even better, thanks to contacts here in Bangkok, they were soon met by new friends who as we speak are taking them to church.

Yesterday we were at a Japanese meeting and one of the songs in the service was "How Great Thou Art." My eyes teared up when I looked at the top of the page and read, "Swedish Folk Song." How true, how Great is our God. Such a wonderful family, with a wonderful hope for new lives. Please continue to pray for the parents, that they are still alive and can someday be rescued.

Marsha

Do not be terrified by them, for the LORD your God, who is among you, is a great and awesome God.
(Deuteronomy 7:21)

55. A Good Place to Pout
(July 25th)

This last Friday, Tony and I went down to the closest beach here in Thailand to check it out for a church excursion (and hopefully baptism; please pray?). We stayed in a nice little guest house and while we were there, I saw something I didn't believe still existed.

What I saw was what I believed to be an extinct form of confident discipline. A nice family with two little boys were lingering around the dining room after breakfast, where there was a hockey game as well as a pool table. The two year old climbed up on a chair and began to fiddle around with the hockey game. The dad went over and began to help him play as well as probably guarding his safety. Then the four year old ran over to try his hand at the pool table, and proceeded to 'pitch a fit' to get his father's attention.

That's where it got interesting. The father, in a level tone, said to the four year old, "We'll play that game soon, but first we're going to enjoy this one. If that doesn't suit you, you're welcome to sit on this bench."

We've all heard this line of discipline before, but the part I thought was extinct surprised me was when the four year old made a face, and went immediately over to the bench and sat down.

They continued to play Hockey for a minute or two, and then the four year old got off the bench, joined in and they all three had a good time before moving on to the pool table.

As I drank my coffee, I had to realize that in a lot of ways, this could touch on what has been our story these past few months. We were having fun in our own adventure, reaching the Japanese with the Gospel right here in Thailand, but now the Board and (hopefully) the Lord have asked us to join in another 'game'. We were treated fairly and kindly, but we found that sitting on the bench was a good place to pout.

Later, when I complimented the boys' Dad for his even discipline, he said, "Oh sure, eventually they get bored on the bench and join in."

While we may have 'pitched a fit' and chosen the bench, the Savior/Father has been kind and loving and is now ready to welcome us into His Game... Japan. We are actually beginning to get excited about moving there in just a few months.

On a completely different note, we are delighted that our little refugee kids are settled and loving it! Safety is such a great feeling... right up there with Freedom.

Love ya,

Marsha

"For we fix our eyes not on what is seen, but what is unseen, for what is seen is temporary but what is unseen is eternal." (2 Corinthians 4:18)

56. Diamonds and Stones
(August 1st)

I remember a song John Denver used to sing a long time ago. It spoke to me then and still does. The title is "Some Days are Diamonds, Some Days are Stones". I won't say this has been a "rocky" week, but we've had our share of both!

Lots of stones. Churches that don't seem to be moving in the direction we want them to go, bills that won't pay themselves, a lovely couple with a sick child, starting down an uncertain road we know only too well...

But in all fairness, there have been a few diamonds as well. Last night we had the privilege of spending the evening with some of Japan's elite: the movers and shakers in both business and politics. Most of them are not Christians, but both Tony and I were so blessed to be drawn into deep conversations with men and women who are honestly seeking God's truth, but until now had had no opportunity to talk to anyone about it. One of them came to church today and afterwards expressed pure joy at what he had heard!

Today we celebrated our Forty First wedding anniversary! How blessed we are to be more in love than when we were just babies by comparison and thought we knew everything about each other! Because it's Sunday and we've just come from seven hours of church, we'll probably save the big celebration for later! But let me say now, "Thank you Lord for watching over us and our marriage all these years."

I guess I'll sum up this week with the following quote by one of our refugee kids who has gone off to a whole new country with a new language, new status and a new name. What he wrote us in his not-so-bad English pretty much says it all: "I love the place where my soul belong to."

Would that we could all be so "diamond directed." Have a good week; I'm sure we will.

Marsha

Husbands, love your wives, just as Christ loved the church and gave himself up for her. In this same way, husbands ought to love their wives as their own bodies. He who loves his wife loves himself.
(Ephesians 5:25 – 28)

Wives, submit to your husbands, as is fitting in the Lord. (Colossians 3:18)

57. The Story of a Boy
(August 8th)

Today we're sort of in transition. Tomorrow we leave for Australia where our little girl is turning 21! We've opted to do it "Australian style" with the sit down dinner, and maybe even a 'surprise guest' or something... who knows. Then we're running around for about a week, preaching at our home church, paying bills, seeing the tax guy, getting driver's licenses renewed, catching up with the Japanese in Australia and doing all the things you do when you're only home every year or so!

So today and next week, I want to tell you a story. Some of this I've known for years, some only recently.

His name was Naoki Noguchi. He was a Japanese boy from a good family and had been conscripted into the Imperial army and was now training to be a "Kamikaze." He turned 17 years when WWII ended. When we asked him what he thought about as he trained, he said it was all 'great fun' for a young boy with no concept of reality or death. He and his friends would laugh and joke about how they were going to die, and how the girls would come for years afterward to Yasukuni Shrine to worship their spirits. Before Naoki could actually start flying, the country ran out of planes, so they searched for other ways to use their Kamikaze troops. They rigged some torpedoes, so that a person could actually get inside one and drive it into the enemy ships. Once inside, the heavy door was bolted down, leaving the driver with no light and just enough air to get to the target. They would steer by means of a radio transmitter that signaled one beep for left and two beeps for right. They practiced on dry land, trying to hit an imaginary target every day. As the tide of the war started turning, the authorities finally decided that, once the driver was sure the torpedo would hit the target, he could honorably get out and swim. The Japanese were having to think about saving their remaining soldiers, since they were beginning to be low on those as well. Naoki laughed as he said, "As if we would have any place to swim to!"

After another little while, they ran out of torpedoes, so Naoki was given a backpack full of explosives and he was stationed along the beach with orders to wait until the enemy was close, then run up to them and detonate the explosives. Then as a second thought, the authorities said that, well, he wouldn't actually have to blow himself up, as long as he could throw the backpack. Again, Naoki laughed as he mimicked trying to get the enemy to wait while he unbuckled the straps on his backpack.

So the boys waited, day after day in hiding places up and down the coastline. One morning he awoke to the sound of Japanese warplanes streaking out to sea. A little later, he heard them coming back, but was dismayed to discover that they were not Japanese Zeroes, but American Corsairs. One flew right along the beach so low and so slow that Naoki could look into the cockpit and see the face of the pilot. His friend to his left took a few potshots at the plane, whereupon it banked right, circled around and opened up with all six guns, shredding his friend's position into ribbons. Naoki raised his gun to shoot, then thought better of it.

"That is when the war finally became real to me," he says now, 70 years later. The image moves me to tears, to think of those two boys, on opposite sides, both scared out of their wits, fighting for something they barely understood themselves.

Thankfully, the war ended and the rest is History. I'm not writing this today because August 6th was the 65th anniversary of the atomic bomb on Hiroshima... that was a terrible thing for both sides, and we feel this deeply because we actually know personally some people who experienced that holocaust up close and personal. But I must say, even most Japanese will say the bomb was necessary to stop the madness. I wrote about the war today because I want to remind us that war hurts everyone, but, like everything else, sometimes God has a way of using a horrible thing to make a good thing. Next week, I'll tell you about the rest of the story, and

how and why we know Noguchi "Sensei" today. Stay tuned, it gets interesting!
Marsha

And we know that in all things God works for the good of those who love him, who have been called according to his purpose. (Romans 8:28)

58. The Rest of the Story
(August 15th)

Ok, I promised you the 'rest of the story' about Noguchi Sensei last week. If you didn't read the blog, please do. So the war ends, and there he was on the furthest southern island of Japan. Somehow he has made contact with his family. His father had been practicing law in Manchuria with his mother and younger brother. Dad told Mom to 'run for her life' when the war was over, as the occupied Manchurians had some very strong anti-Japanese feelings. They fled, leaving the Senior Mr. Noguchi behind. The story sort of breaks up here, but Mom and little brother (about 10 or 11, I think) finally got passage on a ship and made it to the island of Kyushu. Little brother was told he could take ONE thing that he felt was dear to him, and that happened to be a Shoji set, which is like our chess. Because the sailors desperately wanted something to do while the boat sailed languorously along, they would barter for time on the Shoji set by giving the Noguchi family food. Finally they met up with Naoki (our Noguchi, now about 17), and I'm sure the reunion was sweet. Some time later the Dad reached safety, but he had suffered such a harrowing trip, he died almost immediately, mostly from starvation.

Now the story gets interesting...

The remaining Noguchi family, Mom, oldest son Naoki and little brother began the long, long trip by rail to the NORTH of Japan. Why? Because that is the 'homeplace' of the clan and where Father would have to be buried. While Mom sat with the Urn of her husband on her lap, the days and hours passed. Finally they reached the sprawling war torn city of Tokyo. By then they had very little money; only about enough to buy a few sweet potatoes or some other snack as they waited for the train to leave and continue for another day or so until they reached their destination. Mom asked Noguchi to get off and buy something that would sustain them for the rest of the journey. He did.

As he wove thru the alleys of what was called "Ameyoko" for "American Alley"... or the black market, he came across a man shouting about eternal life and such. He stopped to listen, and was delighted when the man explained to him that for just the amount of money he held in his hand, he could have the book that would answer all of his questions.

You guessed it, he returned to the train, not with food, but a Bible. I asked Mom years later what she thought about that. She said sweetly, "He was the oldest son, so my life was in his hands". They proceeded on to Yonezawa, where they had the requisite funeral and burial and set up Mom in the family home. Noguchi opted to return to the southern island, where for some reason he believed he might be able to get a job. Maybe he could even learn to speak English and get a better job. He took the Book with him.

The only English teacher in town was an old Baptist Missionary. She taught once a week and at the end of the lesson, gave an invitation for anyone to ask Jesus into their hearts. Noguchi was a good student, and was reading the Book he had bought, but he held out on the commitment, even though now he remembers whenever he read the Bible he felt at peace.

Finally there was no one left in the class to accept Christ except Noguchi, but the invitation continued every week until one day, he finally gave in and asked Jesus into his lonely heart. Immediately things began to look up and he wrote an excited letter to his mother. "Mom, I've found the answer. Please go to the nearest church and find somebody to explain this to you!" he commanded. She did as she was told, but didn't enjoy the service at all, and furthermore found the people pushy and 'unJapanese'. She didn't plan to return, but the following Sunday, the church members came to her door, beat on a drum and shouted, "Noguchi san! Come to our church like you did last week!" thoroughly mortifying her.

Always the polite Japanese lady and not wanting to

offend, she did go back, and one day she showed the pastor a letter Noguchi had sent. It said something to the effect of "I thank God every day that I bought that Bible on August 8th at Ueno station..."

The pastor read the letter, went a little bit white and handed it back slowly saying, "Look, I can't prove it, but I was definitely selling Bibles that day in Ueno... along the street in Ameyoko!"

The rest is history. Mrs. Noguchi became a Christian immediately. Her son went on to graduate from university and seminary at our Baptist school and has pastored, along with his lovely wife and mother for these many many years. He is now 85, and after both his wife and Mother died, (she was 102), he decided to move into a nursing home rather than obligate his children when he got older. He sold everything in preparation, but right before he went, he thought, "Wait, my 'use by date' has not expired!" So he RETURNED to the North and has taken up residence in the loft of a little church he and his wife helped to build. Tony hopes to write his full story after we move back to Japan next year.

Isn't it fun trusting God, even when we only have enough money for a sweet potato!

Marsha

However, as it is written: "No eye has seen, no ear has heard, no mind has conceived what God has prepared for those who love him." (1 Corinthians 2:9)

59. A Big Week; A Bigger Life
(August 22nd)

Daughter Nicki here. As my parents are on their way home and have had such a big week, I thought I would take this opportunity to tell you a little bit about my story and my thoughts. This week I have had so much fun celebrating my 21st birthday. With the surprise visit of my grandpa, along with my parents, my loving brother and sister in law, and the cutest nephew of all, it was the best party ever, reminiscing over the past 21 years of my life. As I listened to my Dad give his speech, memories of my childhood came back, and I cherish them more every day.

For the past 18 years, I have been lucky to call myself a Woods girl. I have had many opportunities within my life that most people my age have only dreamed of, and for that I am truly thankful. My journey started off in Russia where I was born and dropped at an orphanage in the little town of Armivir. Three years later, my parents found and adopted me and I was brought into a family I could call my own.

"Change" has been a byword throughout my life. From the aftermath of an Armenian Earthquake to snowy Northern Japan, to the beautiful beaches of Gold Coast Australia, I have been through a lot, and often think about my life and its purpose. From those who loved me, starting all the way back in Russia to the beautiful friends and family I cherish now, God has truly blessed me. I have grown up surrounded by wonderful places God has shown me. He has helped me through lots of stages of life, always being a foreigner and the odd one out, whether we're in Japan, Hong Kong, and even America and Australia. I've experienced lots of different schools in different countries including homeschooling with my mother and English speaking schools in Australia where my identity was something I searched for and God helped me find.

Today I'm in university, and I find myself looking into the depth of a huge lake, where many different opportunities and plans lay ahead of me. As I study to become a nurse, my true love of caring for people has become stronger and stronger and I can't wait to see where my future will lead me. With change being a huge part of my life, I feel as though God may be calling me to move into different directions of study but to what direction is still to be seen.

While I have the opportunity, I would like to thank everyone for your prayers and for being there for me during hardships. Thank you for being a great supportive network and for being such wonderfully encouraging people. The love and guidance you have all shown has helped me to realize that in all our experiences, the good times and the bad, we learn from our amazing God, and we learn that our Lord will never give more then what we can handle.

My life verse is more precious to me today than ever before: Jeremiah 29:11,

"For I know the plans I have for you declares the Lord, plans not to harm you, plans to prosper you, and to give you a hope and a future".

Have a wonderful week everyone and God Bless
Nicki

60. From the Vacuum
(August 29th)

Hello there, every one of you faithful readers! We're back in the saddle after a lovely time in Australia. As you know, it was our daughter's 21st, which for some unknown reason, is bigger than graduation or many other of life's passages. You can draw your own conclusions as to why this event is so important; I'm thinking maybe there's a commercial sense.

Married, graduated or not, just about EVERYBODY turns 21, so let's be sure to make THAT the pull-out-the-stops day. On top of that, I was totally surprised to be thrown a surprise 60th birthday party! I don't think I've ever "not seen that coming" in my life, and it was really wonderful. All said, the trip was great, and now we're back, loving Bangkok and all the heat, humidity, traffic, rats in the ceiling... and exciting and faithful Japanese. We feel blessed to have such an absorbing challenge.

Somebody told Tony a blonde joke recently and he loves it. The blonde was asked, "If you spoke in a vacuum, could anybody hear you? She replied, "It probably depends on whether the vacuum is on or off". Personally, I don't get it, but... it is certainly something to think about. I heard a number of people say recently, "I just wish God would tell me what to do... I wish He wasn't so QUIET".

I guess with economic downturns and the state of the world today, it seemed to be almost the main topic of conversation. To this, all I can say is "Join the Club!"

There are so many unresolved issues in most of our lives, and I'm finding out and am somewhat comforted that I'm not alone. I speak and speak to God about all the issues, and... seemingly nothing. Our kids are wonderful and make me proud every day, but they certainly have their dramas. Not big ones, just little "Why is this so difficult, knowing what the next step is?" kind of questions. And it doesn't get any better with age, does it? We're still wondering what our own future will look like, and what we'll become.

We still vacillate between "We love Thailand and the Thais, and are having a fulfilling time here", to "We need to get back to Japan and see if and how we can help the situation there." On the days when we seem to understand or have a good feeling about that question, we tend to head off on tangents, like "How has my parenting damaged my kids?" That's always a good one if you want something to ferment on.

I've been trying to read thru the book of Jeremiah in my quiet time lately. You gotta love poor ole' Jeremiah. 54 chapters prophesying what God is going to do to Israel, with a chapter or two of Jeremiah ranting at God because He still hasn't done it! HOW FRUSTRATED must he have been! How Silent was God concerning Jeremiah's own understanding of what the future looked like? And yet, Jeremiah hung in there till the last. Even when he wavered and worried, got thrown in the well and generally abused, it always came back to what he says in Jeremiah 20: 9,

"But if I say "I will not mention Him or speak any more in His name, His Word is in my heart like a fire, a fire shut up in my bones. I am weary of holding it in; indeed I cannot."

We used to have a poster that said, "If you cannot hear God in the silence, you'll never hear Him when He speaks." Ouch!

Have a good week just abiding in His Love, felt or unfelt, even if the vacuum may be on!

61. Happy Fathers Day!
(September 5th - From Tony)

Today is Father's Day in Australia, so for my gift, Marsha's letting me write this week's blog.
All in all, it couldn't have been a better day, starting with early morning calls from both the kids. I'm told that six-month-old grandson Isaac gave his dad a big bar of Toblerone chocolate, but I guess I'll be content with the calls. Next item on the menu was church with our Japanese folks, and that was memorable. We celebrated Father's Day by holding a "Baby Blessing Day" for the three youngest folk in the group. I said a few words, then Marsha gave each child a candy necklace (Well, not candy, actually, but breakfast cereal wrapped in brightly colored cellophane "beads"). Then at the end of the service, the parents of one of the babies said they would both like to be baptized! We may have mentioned this couple to you before; she's Thai and he's Japanese. He came to my house not long ago looking for peace. He said, "I'd like to believe, but I just have so many questions, and besides, what would happen to my wife (who wasn't a Christian) if I did something like that?" I thought about it a bit, then said, "What you need is a wake up call from God. Let's pray together and ask God to do something so unheard of in the next

couple of weeks that you'll know it's Him." He agreed, we prayed, and the following Sunday his wife suggested they go to a Thai-speaking church. Her only experience with Christianity had been at our Japanese-speaking service. He agreed, they went, and the first time she heard the Gospel in her own language, she became a believer right there on the spot!

I had told the church earlier this morning about how unique each and every one of us is. Those babies we prayed for today each have a genetic signature that, if we could stretch it out would be six feet of DNA. All the DNA in each of their bodies would line up all the way to the moon and back... 178,000 times. And furthermore, each child is totally unique, totally loved and already assigned a perfect Plan by the Heavenly Father. Wherever those kids go, whatever they do in life, the promise we read in Philippians 1:6 will be fulfilled:

"I am sure that God, Who began this good work in you, will carry it on until it is finished on the Day of Christ Jesus."

All in all, Father's Days just don't get any better than this. I hope your day has been a blessed one as well.
Tony

62. Where Else?
(September 12th)

With all the big changes looming on our horizon ahead, I've been thinking a lot about 'work' and 'life.' If any of you read Oswald Chambers "My Utmost for His Highest", he has a lot to say about work and God in the Sept 11th issue. Anyway, as I was thinking, I remembered our famous predecessor, Lottie Moon, who, for you non-Baptists, is like the 'patron saint' of our foreign mission board. You can probably google her. She once said, "I consider myself immortal until my work here on earth is done." When I first heard that, I remember saying to Tony, "We've got to find more work!"

And now here we are, working a lot and loving it; at the same time feeling the heart strings to go back home and bounce the grandbaby or watch our daughter turn into a young woman. Another part of us is getting excited about the 'mysterious' move to Japan, where we have very little idea of what to expect. Every day we're here in Thailand, however, is a gift from God. Today I've decided to tell you why I love Bangkok, and I'm calling it: "Where else?" Those of you who have ever been here will relate. Where else?

...in a city of 13 million can you hop on a train and meet a friend from language school. He's a Korean Missionary who doesn't speak English so you have to use your textbook Thai to have a chat with him.

...you feel safer riding in a taxi that's hot pink because you know it's from a reliable company.

...you think nothing of wading out your front door, or chasing a huge cockroach around the kitchen, finally giving him credit for tenacity and ushering him out the door.

...or how about leaning against a power pole and getting a jolt of electricity that knocks you back and has your hand throbbing for an hour? You don't report it because all the locals know there's a short in the line, and don't touch it.

...starting to actually miss cooking, because you can eat just about anything off the street (vendors) for just a couple of dollars. But then you start thinking about the things you can't have, like hot scones or Mexican casserole! ...ahhhh

...going to a beautiful hospital where you're met by an English-speaking nurse in a white starched uniform. And then the doctor suggests doing a procedure that anywhere else would require a wait of several days or weeks... and he offers to do it immediately. No waiting for test results, either. I had an angiogram last Friday. (I'm fine apparently)

...realizing that any clothing from above about size ten

in this country can't be bought and often you're laughed out of the door for even asking.

watching employees at the bank or post office laughing and teasing each other. Thais work 12 hour days, but they love to have fun while they're doing it.

...marveling at the traffic, usually stopped, while motorcycle taxis weave calmly in and out between the cars, occasionally bumping the passenger's knees or side mirrors of other cars. But rarely ever do you see anyone getting impatient or irritated. A hot temper is considered a liability reserved for foreigners.

Where else? The list could go on and on. The Thai people really earn their description, "The Land of Smiles"...

What a beautiful place to live and work.

We pray that your week is also filled with smiles and thankfulness for the place you are and the job you do. Talk to you again next week!

Marsha

Like cold water to a weary soul is good news from a distant land. (Prov. 25:25)

63. Value
(September 19th)

I met a couple of interesting people this week.
The first one had just had her very first ride in an air conditioned bus in order to come and speak to a group of us ladies in Bangkok. Speaking through an interpreter, she introduced herself as 'Mam'. She's a second year seminary student at a mission school in northern Thailand. She's about four and half feet tall, 90 pounds soaking wet, with long dark hair a beautiful smile. She comes from a hill tribe called "H'Tin" and they are a very few of them, scattered through Laos, Thailand and Burma. She has a proper Thai name for the registry, as well as her H'Tin one, but either are probably 14 or 15 letters long, so even her family calls her 'Mam"

She began by telling us of her life in a refugee camp where she was born. I'm not sure we westerners can really appreciate how terribly desperate a displaced people can be, where because of constant conflict with neighboring tribes, they are forced to flee for their lives. My family and I had experienced a taste of this in an Ethiopian refugee camp a few years ago, and H'Tin's story really brought back some memories. She described her life as "safe," but we need to understand that her definition means simply that she has a shelter of some sort and a limited supply of food.

These people are so marginalized, and although the Thai government offered to help, the place they were given to live was far from livable, located deep and unreachable in what she calls a 'forest'. There was no school, no infrastructure of any kind. She soon had nine brothers and sisters and so the saga of her life continued. Finally some missionaries came to her telling her and her family of a "Heavenly Father who loved them". Many believed, including Mam. Then, one day, when she was about 14, someone offered her a better life in a dormitory where she could also attend school. A girl going to school was unheard of (remember this would have been only about five or ten years ago) but she was able to go. There she excelled, because even though she'd never even ridden a bus or seen a two-story building, she really is a smart little girl. Before long, she had finished five or six years of school and was able to pass a high school exam. (In a new language, Thai). Then, wonder of wonders, someone paid her tuition for SEMINARY! It only costs $600 a year including room and board, but with a family of 11, who at best probably only has an annual wage of a couple hundred dollars, that is beyond comprehension. Now she's in her second year, and she has not been back to see her family in two years because she doesn't have the five dollars for the bus ride. But she knows how proud of her they are, and that keeps her going. Her goal is to be a music evangelist, sharing with others like herself the love of Jesus.

The second man I met this week is a Japanese missionary to the Thai. He and his family have been in Thailand for 15 years, loving children in the slums and telling them what he wasn't able to tell his friend when he was about ten yrs old. Apparently this friend had overheard his parents discussing his poor test scores and squabbling about whose fault it was. The words "worthless" and "I wish he'd never been born" fell on this little boy's ears. A few days later this boy asked his best friend, (who would later become this pastor, "Do you think my life has value?" What could this guy say in return, what does any ten year old know about value? The friend answered, "I don't know, but you're my friend and that's valuable to me!" Several days later the sad little boy was hit on his bicycle and he died, knowing only that his friend thought he was important. It wasn't till years later when the pastor first found Christ and read in Isaiah 43:4, "...you are precious and honored in my sight... I love you...," that he could shout out to his long gone but not forgotten friend, "You are Loved by God! You truly had value!"

Value...............Love..............people who seemingly have no hope and no 'value' to others, are so very important and so loved by God. Our daily prayer is that all of those people get a chance to experience knowing their worth in God's eyes.

Mam finished her talk to us with this quote. Later I asked her if it was a H'Tin saying or a famous proverb and she just smiled and said, "Oh no, I just thought of it."

"Lord, let me never use my strengths to harm others or my weaknesses to harm myself." Now THAT has VALUE, don't you think?

Love you,

Marsha

64. Who Am I
(September 26th)

We'll be on the road when this usually goes out, and Nicki's computer has crashed (she usually sends it for us), so you'll be getting this early.

My friend Oswald Chambers said something interesting in his book, "My Utmost for His Highest" again this week. His theme lately seems to be dealing with the ideas of "call" and "duty". He says, "The important thing to God is not what you DO; it's who you ARE." That comes as a great relief for us during those times when we feel we haven't really DONE much for the cause... or worse yet, when we feel that what we HAVE done, is not worth much to the Kingdom.

But let me say, this has been a good week. I even told Tony, "I feel like we're being led through these fantastic times of harvest because there must be a famine coming!"

For example, on Tuesday, we sat with the couple who have both decided to be baptized soon. We wrote a blog some months ago (June 20th) about him struggling with his troubled marriage and his unbelief in God. He prayed with Tony that 'something amazing' would happen in the next week, just to show him that there really IS a God who cares... and a few days later his wife heard the Gospel for the first time in her own language and became a Christian! Tuesday as they sat on our couch, smiling and whispering back and forth, we were reminded how Christ can heal hearts as well as save souls. She only speaks Thai and a little English, he speaks Japanese and only a little Thai, so it was an interesting conversation to say the least. Please pray for them as they write their "Shinko kokohakus," a testimony to what God has done in their lives, and why they want to be baptized. Stay tuned...

Then Wednesday we got a letter from Japan. Apparently one of our students from literally YEARS ago has written a book which is getting rave reviews in Japan. In the early 80's this guy had wandered into one of our youth groups, became a Christian, and sometime later, Tony took him to visit some friends of his in what's called a 'bed school'. (In other words, a place where you drop off and forget your kid for his whole life because he was unfortunate enough to have muscular dystrophy). Tony enjoyed meeting with those young men with the bright minds trapped in disabled bodies. Over the years, he would often take new Christians out there as part of their discipleship.

Anyway, this old student friend has grown up, become a professor and has now written a book about one of the patients who became a Christian. He had the best life he could have had considering he had Muscular Dystrophy, doing some amazing things for the Lord until his death a couple of years ago. Hearing about these friends, and being reminded of those precious years with all those young men with all-too-short lives, Tony and I are humbled. We never wanted to do anything more than touch lives, and now we're finding that God has touched so many around us, in spite of what we happened to be doing and in spite of what we may have been thinking about what we were doing at the time.

You're so right, Brother Oswald, it's not what you do; it's what you are that counts for the Kingdom. And that has nothing whatsoever with what we've done, but everything about Who He IS.

Love ya,

Marsha

Since you are precious and honored in my sight, and because I love you, I will give men in exchange for you, and people in exchange for your life. Do not be afraid, for I am with you; I will bring your children from the east and gather you from the west. (Isaiah 43:4-5)

65. Rules
(October 3rd)

Last Sunday we slipped away after church to go check out a little guest house down south on the beach. While Thailand has some fabulous places to stay (with accompanying fabulous prices), there are also some 'cheaper' places that I thought we should check out before we take a small mission team there soon. We stayed in one of these places before; I'm not sure how many 'stars' it was, but I remember waking up after a rather uncomfortable night and having to wait till my eyes focused to ascertain that there was indeed a giant slug smiling up at me from my toothpaste tube! Now I rate some of these beach bungalows by SLUGS instead of STARS.

Anyway, the place we picked this time was OK, and so we decided to take in a nearby cave that was being touted as a great tourist attraction. After a HOT and sweaty climb up a mountain, we came to a hole in the ground with some Thai writing on it, and a rickety ladder going into the abyss. Fortunately, some locals had given us flashlights, so we gingerly started down... into the pitch black. On hands and knees, we crawled through the cave from one "cathedral" to another, each connected by a low passage marked only with a small arrow scratched into the wall. Eventually we came into a large cavern filled with BATS. Tony and I both freaked out and started crawling back out. It was an orderly retreat, I think, but how did I manage to crawl over Tony three times on the way out?

Safely exited, and starting down the mountain towards the car, we compared this cave to others we've visited. It occurred to us that we've never been in a cave alone, and never but NEVER been allowed to touch anything. In this cave, not only was touching permitted, but absolutely essential, since only the stalactites offered any support while climbing down the slippery slopes. We've always had rules upon rules, and we realized, that was somewhat of a relief. Somehow the complete absence of any kind of control was frankly a little scary. "You want to lean over that bottomless pit? Go ahead! Who's stopping you?" And of course with no 'public friendly' preparation, we missed a lot which might have been much more enjoyable, such as whole caverns full of beautiful views, but invisible to all but the strongest flashlight. Worn down nubs along the way served as reminders that there used to be some really great formations, but unfortunately have long since been hauled out by less scrupulous visitors.

We decided that life is like that. Rules help. Last week we got that phone call that every Dad hopes for and yet dreads at the same time. It's an old rule and we felt honored when he called. Two men struggled for conversation, but at the end of it, a fine young suitor asked for Nicki's hand in marriage. We are delighted; he's a wonderful boy, a strong Christian, and best of all, he still carries that respect for rules which seem to have been all but forgotten these days.

This morning, he proposed in the best possible place and in the best possible way: in church, before witnesses and surrounded by Christian family who love and support them both. Who could ask for more? Please pray for Nicki and Chris as they enter this new stage of life. Pray especially that they'll move smoothly thru this transition to marriage, and pray that they can endure the long engagement they seem to be planning.

Thank you Lord for giving us rules to live by... because sometimes a few rules make everything feel secure.

Love ya,

Marsha

The precepts of the LORD are right, giving joy to the heart. The commands of the LORD are radiant, giving light to the eyes. (Psalms 19:8)

66. Love a Challenge
(October 10th)

Well, as you probably know if you're on Facebook, it's been an exciting week. The daughter is well and truly proposed to/engaged and all is sailing along in a flurry of excitement. Stay tuned.

On that note, Tony has now led his FIRST ever MEN's group in our little Japanese Church in Thailand. There was a great turnout, and ended with promises to carry on the tradition, even after we leave for Japan. In preparing for the meeting, he was trying to think of some way to appeal to the knuckle dragging, chest beating, testosterone motivated sensibilities of the male side of the room when he came across this ad from a 1913 London newspaper. Maybe you've seen it as well:

"Men wanted for Hazardous Journey. Small wages, bitter cold, long months of complete darkness, constant danger, safe return doubtful. Honour and recognition in case of success."

Would you have answered an ad like that? I certainly wouldn't have, but then I'm not a man, which was Tony's point when he shared it with the group of men last night. In fact, over a thousand men responded to Ernest Shackleton's call for an expedition to the Antarctic.

Let's face it, men LIKE adventure! As a part of his

presentation to the men last night, he asked such questions as, "Would you rather play a harp or shoot a gun? Pet a baby seal or wrestle a bear?" I don't even need to tell you what kind of answers he got. And with that in mind, why is it that most churches worldwide are made up of a majority of women? Of course there are lots of reasons, but part of it is the sad fact that men look at the Gospel and don't see the adventure that is there. Those men last night resolved to bring danger back into the church. I'm worried, but stay tuned.

Men do love a challenge. Why else would Chris propose to Nicki? Marriage is a challenge, going to the south pole is a challenge, staying pure in this generation is a challenge, telling a lost and hurting world that Jesus loves them is a challenge. (Don't tell anyone but we women have a bit of adventurous streak in us as well, don't you think?)

Please pray for us in the coming weeks as we face some 'challenging' events. Leaving a very small but faithful church to what we don't know... we're not sure we'll "SUCCEED" in the terms of what we chose to call success. Saying good bye to Thailand (OK OK we still have a few months, but the sadness is already creeping in). Thinking about giving our daughter away, which someone described as giving a Stradivarius violin to a 500 pound gorilla.

I know you know what I mean, and could add a few things to the list as well. Be assured that we'll be praying for you as well. Give us some prayer points, won't you?
Love ya,
Marsha

I have been constantly on the move. I have been in danger from rivers, in danger from bandits, in danger from my own countrymen, in danger from Gentiles; in danger in the city, in danger in the country, in danger at sea; and in danger from false brothers.
I have labored and toiled and have often gone without sleep; I have known hunger and thirst and have often gone without food; I have been cold and naked.
Besides everything else, I face daily the pressure of my concern for all the churches. (2 Corinthians 11:26 – 28)

67. Soul Mates
(October 17th)

This week has rocked along quietly for us. Our son Nathan and lovely wife Kylie celebrated their fourth anniversary, this time with a little bundle of joy and interrupter of romance, Isaac Trevor. It's such a joy just watching him grow, and the interruption doesn't seem so irritating, at least not to us, who can turn off Skype and walk away! Ha

As the seasons change in most of the places you live, either to summer or winter, we're enjoying the same enduring HEAT, although it seems to rain much more than necessary lately. Guess that's why they call it the 'rainy season' for lack of any better explanation.

I had an interesting and recurring experience this last week. I met a lady who I felt like I've known all my life but actually had never met. The Japanese would call it 'fate' but I prefer to call it "God's timing." In 1979 when we were first appointed to Japan, we were slated to go all the way to the south island of Kyushu and teach in our big Baptist university, Seinan Gakkuin. We would be spending all our free time in what was called a 'friendship house,' befriending the students and introducing the Gospel to them. This lady I mentioned apparently had just graduated from the University and was the secretary there. We would have worked with her.

But like so many of 'our' plans, things didn't work out, and we didn't go to Kyushu, but rather about the same distance to the NORTH to a town called Sendai, where we spent the best part of our lives, doing basically the same thing, showing students the amazing love of Christ. We never crossed paths with this particular lady, and the rest is history.

Then this last Friday I met her here in Bangkok. This was the weekend set aside to celebrate the life our Japanese church's late pastor, Kondo Sensei. We were impressed to see several former members who had flown in from Japan, Vietnam, and the Philippines to participate in his memorial. We didn't really have time to get to know Kondo Sensei before he died a few months ago. Tony has stepped in to fill the gap until the church can find a new pastor, but we gather he was a great and well loved man. Tony preached the memorial service today and it was very touching.

I was struck by something this previously unknown lady said. She and her husband had been living and working in Bangkok for a few years before going back to Japan 18 months ago. As "fate" would have it, they missed us by one month, since we got here just after they left. At a "pre memorial" dinner on Friday night, she said, "We came in tonight, saw everybody and just took up talking, like we'd only been gone for a week or so. That's the beauty of Christian friendship, isn't it!"

I agree. I feel like I've only been apart from this lady a week or so, when in reality we'd never even met her! It was only our shared history on common ground that drew us together. Only God can tune hearts together like this!

I pray that you have many 'soul mates' in Christ. It makes us all look forward to meeting the 'others' in heaven, doesn't it?

Have a good week,

Marsha

A man of many companions may come to ruin, but there is a friend who sticks closer than a brother.
(Proverbs 18:24)

68. Bigger Bags
(October 24th)

"Please pray for Tony Sensei; he's so sick, with a fever of 37.8 (99)" ...the letter ran on and on, adding, "And Marsha Sensei is also sick, so they really need our prayers."

That letter came to us this week, and to every other member of the Japanese church, and maybe to you too! Japanese get alarmed when their leaders are not in top form.

As it was, Tony ate something and had a bad night, struggling with food poisoning (common here) and then, probably because of lack of sleep, spiked a little fever that lasted about a day. This does not constitute sickness in Bangkok, but as I said, the Japanese like to worry about their leaders. It's sweet to be loved but it was just that, nothing more. I'm not sure why I was also listed as ill, but maybe they thought I had sympathetic pains.

As a result we decided (since we were evidently sick) to take a couple of days and go to the beach with some old friends from Japan, as well as our friends who work in the student center here in Bangkok. It actually IS a holiday here, so off we went.

HOW wonderful Thailand can be! The place we went

was almost completely deserted, the food was good, the company great, and the rest and fresh air was nice as well.

Yesterday as I walked along the beach, all alone, just enjoying the beauty, I started picking up shells. Finally my hands were full, but there were still more beautiful shells to procure. I stopped to chuckle when I remembered an incident that happened to my Father-in-Law, Buddy, years ago.

They were missionaries living in Taiwan, and when they could take a holiday, Dad liked to walk along the deserted beach at a place called Olanbi, picking up the glass fishing floats that had broken away from nets off shore and found their way to the beach. He still has several of these today. You've probably seen them; usually they're greenish glass sometimes encased in a holder made of rope.

He found several that day, but he was hoping to find a really big one; or at least bigger than the one his friend had found and had been bragging about. As he walked along, he began a conversation with the Lord, and as they talked, it became more something along the line of "I'd really, really like one of those big ones, Lord." "If You really loved me, You'd let me find a big one!"

He grumbled along, thinking of his sad fate, when suddenly he caught a glimpse of sparkling green off in the distance. Hurrying over, he found it: the really, really big one he was hoping for. Struggling to squeeze it into the plastic grocery bag he had brought along, he said, "This is great Lord! Thank you. ….But you know, I think the one my friend found might be just a tad bigger…"

At that point, God spoke to Buddy's heart, just as clearly as if He were standing beside him in the flesh. He spoke only seven words, but those words spoke volumes: "You could have brought a bigger bag."

How many times is my faith like that? I ask for a harvest but have no way of dealing with it when it comes. I grumble, when in fact, I'm not prepared.

I too, left the beach yesterday with fewer shells than I wanted, but only because I had no way of carrying more.

"The harvest is plentiful but the workers are few."
(Matthew 9:27)

Something to think about!
Love ya,
Marsha

69. Cosmetics
(October 31st)

If you've ever been to Bangkok, you'll know that there are some pretty obnoxious smells around. Maybe it's the heat, or the often open sewers... I don't know. Yesterday, while visiting a nearby slum, I sat beside a klong (canal) that literally took my breath away. It was a relief to notice the Thai people sitting with me were also struggling with the smell.

But all that is to say, in spite of the difficult living conditions, here are some of the most BEAUTIFUL people, especially women, I've seen anywhere. I try to figure if this is because the two top selling (at least advertised) things around amongst the classy elite, or "High So" as they're called (short for "high society"), seem to be prune juice and scotch broth (beef bullion). Add to that bird's nest soup as you get older, and how could you help but be beautiful?

All kidding aside, I'd like to draw you to some 'real beauty' that we see unfolding around here.

First of all, as you may know, I'm teaching about 20 Japanese women a course in "God-led parenting techniques." My own children are amused when they hear I'm preaching about patience and kind words every week; after all, they remember what it was really like at our house! But I'm trying my best to share with these ladies what God wants us to do with our kids. We have two-thirds non-Christian women coming (that's two-thirds of the class, not that the ladies are two-thirds non-Christian… don't you just love the English language?). Anyway, one of the non-Christians said the other day, "This class is sorta like a good skin care product. You put it to use, but it's several weeks before you can begin to see results!"

Let me tell you another cute story. Remember the couple that recently accepted Christ after they went to church to search for answers regarding their crumbling marriage? We baptised him a few weeks ago, and his wife, being Thai, is studying now to be baptised in the Thai church as she doesn't really understand Japanese. Anyway, the other day she said to him "I can't really put my finger on when it was you started looking good to me, but it's happening!" Isn't that the sweetest thing to say after eight years of a very rocky marriage? Isn't Christ's healing power amazing?

Prune Juice, Cosmetics or just the overall LOVE and HEALING of a Savior……………..we all look better!

Love ya too,

Marsha

How beautiful on the mountains are the feet of those who bring good news, who proclaim peace, who bring good tidings, who proclaim salvation, who say to Zion, "Your God reigns!" (Isaiah 52:7)

70. Music and History
(November 7th)

A good friend/opera singer back in Australia once told us, "Music shouldn't be simply good; it should transport you!" Well, last night we were transported. At least 2000 Japanese gathered at the Bangkok Cultural Center for a concert by an ensemble called Euodia. It's made up of six Japanese who play violin, cello, piano and clarinet; everything from Bach to Bob Dylan. I think everyone in the audience was (as the Aussies would say, "gobsmackered"); first that such an insignificant-looking group on a huge stage could produce such a room-filling sound. But what really brought gasps of surprise was when one of the ensemble members came to the microphone to say, "Twenty four years ago, we sat down together. We were all new Christians, and very excited about what God was doing in our lives. We asked ourselves, How can we share this wonderful experience with others? And the answer we came to was: with music. We hope you enjoy this concert tonight. But even more, we hope you sense a bit of the fragrance of God's love." Then they played "Amazing Grace." The audience started singing, in whatever language came from the heart: English, Thai, Japanese...

It was breathtaking. But that was only part of the evening's "transportation". The second half of the concert featured a guest appearance from Japanese singer Chu Kosaka. He and his sidekick, Makoto Iwabuchi were, I believe, personally responsible for bringing contemporary Christian music to Japan, back in the 70's. Until that time, the only music associated with Christianity was from the old traditional hymnbook. Not bad, mind you, but a little un-appreciated by the younger folks. Chu and Makoto brought in guitars and started singing about God's love with a Simon and Garfunkel style that left everyone... well... gobsmackered. Makoto was from Sendai, where we lived and worked for around 20 years, so every time they came there for a concert, we were on the front row. We got to know them personally, and had them in our home several times. Then we lost touch with them.

Last night after the concert, I came up to Chu, shook his hand and said, "The last time we met was 30 years ago. You and Makoto sat around our "kotatsu" and had tea. I handed him our card and said, Marsha and I will be back in Tokyo next January; I hope we can get together and talk about old times."

I'd give an eye tooth for the look on his face. He was transported before our eyes, but in a different way! We look forward to seeing him in Tokyo, and sharing that "fragrance" of God's love again.

Music, history, old friends... it all comes together to

make up that scent of joy and fulfillment. I hope your lives are full of it today. God bless!
Marsha

But thanks be to God, who always leads us in triumphal procession in Christ and through us spreads everywhere the fragrance of the knowledge of him.
(2 Corinthians 2:14)

71. Interesting Question; Surprising Responses
(November 14th)

As you may know, I'm teaching "The Joy of Parenting" to about 20 Japanese mothers. Some are Christian, most are not, but they're all eager to learn about God-guided parenting, so they keep coming back.

We are in our eigth week, and the lesson was about "homeru," the Japanese word for "praise." The gist of the lesson is about encouraging your children to try new things, allowing them the freedom to reach beyond themselves, and then to praise them when they do... that sort of stuff.

Actually, the class was going rather dismally. That morning, if anything could have gone wrong, it did. The pre-class worship session went long and when we got to the room, we were already running late. The video clip that I had so carefully set up had gone into sleep mode and reverted to a password protection that I didn't know. Then, when I finally got it running again, I played the wrong video! The air conditioner was either blasting freezing air or making us all hot. The words I said in Japanese were wrong and I started to lose my confidence. I began to wonder if I was worthy of any "homeru" myself...

Finally, I presented them with the capstone of the lesson, a quote famous among some circles. I wrote it on the board with renewed vigor; this was to be the 'PUNCH LINE" to the lesson. Because I'm lazy and sometimes they enjoy a splash of English, I wrote it like this: "What great thing would you attempt if you knew you couldn't fail?"

Twenty faces stared at me aghast. I knew they might have trouble with this, because most of them have little English skills, so I 'explained' it in Japanese. Of course, just to be safe, I had already asked my friend to be ready with a 'translation' of my poor Japanese in case I needed it. She read her version off with confidence... and they continued to stare. I had her read it again and began to realize that both she and they were in some kind of crisis. I was tempted to speak louder, thinking maybe they'd understand it better if I yelled.

You see, they were hearing this sentence as many a Japanese would, given their education and background. They were reading and understanding... "If you were told to do something, and knew that you would not be ALLOWED to fail, what would you attempt?"

But as I said, I wasn't having the best day anyway, so I kept after them, thinking that if I just persevered, they'd 'get it' and answer me, even though they were looking more and more uncomfortable. Finally a lady on the front row who was given no choice but to answer, said softly and sadly, "I would attempt NOTHING!"

....It was only then that "the penny dropped" and I understood the mistake.

The Japanese were hearing, "If you would NOT BE ALLOWED to fail (ie: it is not permissible to fail) what would you attempt?" And the answer of course would be a resounding "NOTHING!"

We Westerners hear "cannot fail" and rejoice. Nothing we do will be held against us or our failed attempt because we WON'T be failing! Yippee!

Why do we look at this sentence like that? Why was the original author of this sentence such a persuasive preacher of positive thinking? Is it because of God's grace which gives us the freedom to BE everything He has created us to be, without fear of failure?

I think some of my poor ladies are still scratching their heads. I re-worded the sentence and wrote it again on the board, "If you were told to do something, knowing that you were guaranteed success, what would you attempt?" ....Poor things, they were ruined for the day and were still mumbling amongst themselves when I left. Next week, I think I'll start by comparing this last week to parenting, that is, sometimes NOTHING goes right, but you just have to soldier on anyway, praying all the while that there's no permanent damage done. This next

Wednesday, I just hope that the things I attempt to teach them will be met with some degree of success, in God's marvelous grace and mercy using this humble vessel, who is glad she feels free to fail sometimes.

Have a great week and see if you can (be allowed) to attempt great things!

Marsha

Then you will have success if you are careful to observe the decrees and laws that the LORD gave Moses for Israel. Be strong and courageous. Do not be afraid or discouraged. (1 Chronicles 22:13)

72. Float Your Boat
(November 21st)

Tonight as you're reading this, we'll be literally 'floating our boat'. It's called "Loi Kratong" and I'm guessing it's the second biggest festival in Thailand.

If you google it, you'll find countless pictures. Here's the deal: families, companies or individuals make a 'kratong' or a little raft, ranging in size from about the size of a plate to the size of a car. They used to be made of bamboo or banana leaves, but in order to be more environmentally friendly (especially to the fish) they're now mostly made out of bread... really dry hard bread, so they have a chance of floating at least a little ways before they capsize or sink. You decorate it, put things on it, like coins and such, light a candle and set it off into the river. If you can squeeze past the mobs of rowdy and partying people, it's really quite a beautiful sight, as all the lighted floats make their way down the river, of the canal, or even the little pond where we'll be releasing ours.

Now before you think we've joined the heathens, let us explain.

If you've googled the festival, you've discovered that there are a myriad of beliefs about this cultural activity. I've asked several people and gotten different answers, but basically, the main idea is that it's a gift or 'prayer' back to the river, and the spirits thereof, who give them life. The mighty Mekong is not very far away and Bangkok sits on the Chao Praya River, which is equally impressive. In fact, most of Southeast Asia is water orientated. Never mind that only a fool would EVER drink ANY water anywhere, still, without the monsoon rains and the rivers, this huge breadbasket called Asia would be in dire straits. The river means life to everyone. Oh, but back to the beliefs. More than one internet site, and most of the people we've talked to, while agreeing that it's essentially a Buddhist festival to the river, will also add that by floating the "kratong" you are really asking the spirits to (as one source says) "float away ill fortune." They often put fingernails and hair clippings on their little raft, to represent the 'bad' things about their life.

I was reading in Hebrews ten today about how the Jews had to constantly send in a priest every year to atone for their sins. EVERY YEAR. The sins had to be taken away, the 'ill fortune' had to be dealt with, just like here in Bangkok, every year... until Christ came to offer us salvation.

We are acting on the instruction of a progressive Thai pastor, who suggests that we all put a CROSS on our little boat and therefore show that we are proclaiming

Jesus, the Savior that takes away our sins once and for all!
For this we are grateful.
This week is also American Thanksgiving. We will eat with the neighbors and celebrate a life FULL of thanks... and we'll be thinking of you!
Marsha and Tony

The next day John saw Jesus coming toward him and said, "Look, the Lamb of God, who takes away the sin of the world!" (John 1:29)

73. Giving Thanks
(November 28th)

When you read this today, you'll have gotten thru your Thanksgiving festivities in your various countries. I'm encouraged to see more and more "Thanksgivings" popping up in Australia as well. We had a nice little one with the next door neighbors and a Thai Turkey, which, although it was skinny and lean, was surprisingly tasty! As I write you today I'm full of Thanksgiving for two wonderful years in Thailand. We had our last service with the Japanese church and it was beautiful. So many lovely testimonies as to how God has worked in the church, and lots of mostly undeserved affirmations about our part in the whole process. Now we give these folks back to God and trust that they'll stay strong in Him. Fortunately for us, most of them will be passing thru Japan in the years to come and we'll be able to meet up with them. I've finished up my classes with the Japanese women and will truly miss them. They were so much fun, and it was a real blessing to hear their unforgettable comments about God's work in their lives. We are also thankful that Nicki, her fiancé Chris and another 'almost our kids' couple will be boarding a plane as you read this, coming to us for two weeks. We'll spend one week here in Thailand wrapping up our work and sharing this part of our lives with them. Then we all head off to Cambodia for about ten days of work in an orphanage. Should be fun, and I hope a blessing for all. I know you're all busy as the holiday season just keeps on going, and since we're not even sure of where our next internet connection is going to be, I'll sign off for a few weeks.

The next time we get together like this, we'll be back in Japan, after a thirteen year interval, coming home (in the words of John Denver), to a place we've never been before. I suspect the country has changed a lot, and I know we have. Like the Ephesian philosopher Heraclitus said a long time ago, "You can't cross a river twice. The river will be different. You will be different." Praise be to God, that even though we and the places we've lived grow old with the years, HE never changes. His love for us is "the same yesterday, today and tomorrow." That's what I want to leave with you, Dear Reader. Enjoy the journey, sample the sights and smells along the way, and know that at the end of the road, there is a wonderful place for God's children: a place where the sights have never been more beautiful, the fragrance never more breathtaking, and the journey never more worth each step of the way.

Love ya,

Marsha (and Tony)

Other Marton Publishing Devotional Books
Available at martonpublishing.com

The Road Rising - Tony Woods
A one year devotional book which follows the daily journey of a man on a backpack trip. In the course of his journey he encounters fire, storm, loneliness and true friendship throughout his commitment to follow the One who called him to the challenge.

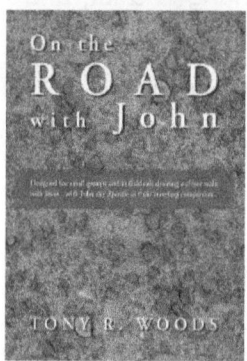

On the Road with John - Tony Woods
A one year study of John's Gospel designed especially for small groups. Each of the fifty two lessons includes a "Road" worksheet which guides the reader through analysis, contemplation and discussion of particular themes within the lesson.

Gathering My Stones - Janet Brooks
An assortment of Bible verses and poems, for those who hold prayers within their souls, but no words to voice them; for those who desire more words of praise, more encouragement, more of God; a glimpse into what could be theirs as children of the King.

Other Marton Publishing Books
Available at martonpublishing.com

A Hope & A Furutre - Marsha N Woods
Born on the heels of the horrific Spitak Earthquake, little Ma'sha had little hope for survival, much less for any kind of joy in her future. But there was a Power over it all with a different kind of plan, from the Russian village of Armavir to a new home and a new future.

Uncle Buddy - Tony Woods
When missionary Buddy Woods' wife passed away, he felt that he would be following her soon. But God had other plans for this faithful vertern of many years of missionary work in Africa and China. Many wonderful stories through his journey of a life making a difference.

Looking for a Lamb - Tony Woods
A father's journey up the mountain of grief and beyond. In this unique analogy which reflects upon Abraham of the Bible, follow the painful ascents of two fathers. Both discover at the summit the only Lamb Who can make sense of the tragedy.

www.ingramcontent.com/pod-product-compliance
Lightning Source LLC
Chambersburg PA
CBHW032110090426
42743CB00007B/306